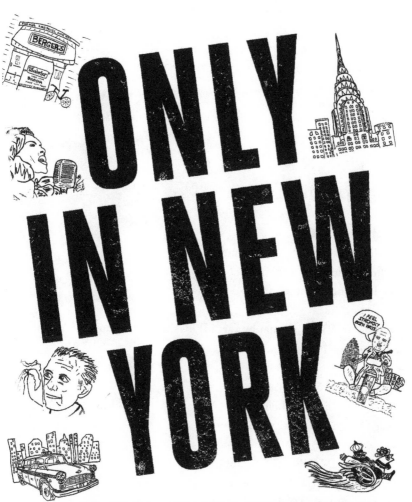

ONLY IN NEW YORK

36 TRUE BIG APPLE STORIES
SPANNING 55 YEARS AND FIVE BOROUGHS

M.G.CRISCI

ORCA PUBLISHING COMPANY USA • 2018

Published in eBook format by Orca Publishing Company, USA
Converted by http//www.eBookit.com

Illustrations by M.G. Crisci
Edited by Robin Friedheim
Cover Design by Good World Media

Amazon KDP ISBN: 978-1-4566-3249-6
Paperback ISBN: 978-1-4566-3248-9
Hardcover ISBN: 978-1-4566-3250-2

Manufactured in the United States of America

First Edition

Also by M.G. Crisci

7 Days in Russia
Call Sign, White Lily
Donny and Vladdy
Indiscretion
Mary Jackson Peale
Only in New York
Papa Cado
Papa Cado's Book of Wisdom
Project Zebra
Salad Oil King
Save the Last Dance
This Little Piggy

Learn more at
mgcrisci.com
twitter.com/worldofmgcrisci
YouTube.com/worldofmgcrisci
Facebook.com/worldofmgcrisci

Foreword

JANUARY 2019

I'm an imperfect being who has lived an imperfect life. Through it all I have loved my New York, the streets, the people, the meter of the place. There is nothing like it anywhere in the world.

I'm also one of the luckiest men on earth. I've had a great life, rich in experiences, and God gave me the gift to organize my thoughts, tell my stories, hopefully in an entertaining manner.

So, after an amazing roller-coaster business career, I found a new passion: creating literary works about real people and real events. After 12 books, a screenplay, and a stage play, I decided I had earned the right to create a book of short stories in a New York state of mind.

Somewhere along the way, I realized this book wasn't just a collection of short stories; it's my life in all its imperfect glory; it's proof that a man named Matt Crisci once passed through here. I hope you enjoy reading it as much as I have enjoyed living it.

One last comment. When I pass, I've asked my family — who now lives in Southern California — one last favor. Would they please take my ashes and toss them to the wind in New York

Harbor as they passed the Statue of Liberty on the Staten Island
Ferry.

M. S. Crisci

Table of Contents

Chapter 1

Uncle Tip-Top and Tony 4
A supervisor at the Wonder Bread Company, with a
thriving Numbers Racket, ponders a replacement hire. 1

Chapter 2

Billy, Whitey, the Mick, and Me
A Yankee Stadium vendor recalls a time when men played
professional baseball for the drunken camaraderie. 5

Chapter 3

Marvin, Where are You?
The lone white kid on a black basketball team remembers
his mentor in trying times. 9

Chapter 4

Y.A. Tittle's Hot Chocolate
A beverage vendor reeks havoc on an NFL fan's new
winter topcoat. 13

Chapter 5

Wedding Night at The Plaza
Two newlyweds inadvertently blow the $4,000 they
collected at their wedding reception. 17

Chapter 6

Buitoni Spaghetti and Abbie Hoffman
Two junior executives learn to eat well without spending a
dime. 25

Chapter 7

World-Famous Baloney Omelets
A Jewish deli sells baloney omelets made by a Japanese
short-order cook served by a Puerto Rican waitress. 29

Chapter 8

Veal and Peas in Brown Gravy
Drunk Brazilian couple and their American friends have
farewell dinner at a snooty, midtown French restaurant. 33

Chapter 9

Footsteps on 47th
A Big Apple visitor gets the scare of a lifetime on the way
to a Broadway show...37

Chapter 10

Coffee Near Carnegie
Offering a shiny silver dollar to a person in need elicits an
unexpected response. 41

Chapter 11

"Hymie, You're Killing Me!"
Two multi-millionaire garmentos haggle over the price of 2
million yards of fabric at the Russian Tea Room. 47

Chapter 12

Ya Shudda Told Me!
Cabbie attempts to scam another New Yorker before
bonding... 51

Chapter 13

30-Ounce Porterhouse
Men in high places exhibit testosterone-laden behavior at a
landmark New York steakhouse..57

Chapter 14

Leonard M.D.
A patient recalls his promise of dinner with his doctor and
their respective families...61

Chapter 15

JELL-O Bowl II

An annual client-agency sporting Olympiad reaches
unfathomable heights. 71

Chapter 16
Time to Say Goodbye
Abandoning normality for the opportunity to become
filthy rich. 77

Chapter 17
Greedy, as Charged
Taking a life-changing roller-coaster ride through the dark
side of Wall Street with the lunatic fringe. 83

Chapter 18
"Hey Everybody, I Know Him!"
An inebriated bum on Third Avenue incorrectly identifies
Mr. Tres Cool in his $6,000 custom-made Saville Row. 87

Chapter 19
Piccarella's Chinatown
Buying fireworks with the kids in the back alleys of
Chinatown 91

Chapter 20
Hubcaps at Fort Apache
A high school student learns you gotta do, what you gotta
do. 97

Chapter 21
"Bruce, Get in the Car"
A businessman, who looks like the twin brother of
Mobster John Gotti's consigliere, receives an unexpected
invitation at 11 PM. 101

Chapter 22
The 6:27 Express

A depressing portrait of commuters traveling into
Manhattan..105

Chapter 23

$132,600 in Six Hours
Office temp and her friends borrow a business executive's
identity and go on a six-hour shopping spree..................109

Chapter 24

Corner Table at La Mela
A restauranteur assumes his patron is a mafia-made man
who prefers the right table, just in case.............................115

Chapter 25

The Return of Meatloaf
A rock icon fulfills a 17-year-old promise at Madison
Square Garden. 119

Chapter 26

Taxi Driver
Taxi driver returns to Vietnam while driving a passenger up
First Avenue..125

Chapter 27

Pearls at Tiffany's
Buying a Valentine's gift at Tiffany & Co. becomes an
enlightening experience. 131

Chapter 28

Sniffen Court
An evening walk offers surprising insights into the lives we
lead..135

Chapter 29

J.L.'s Christmas Tree
A white family racism is alive and well during the
Rockefeller Center Christmas celebration. 141

Chapter 30

Scrambled Eggs, Strawberry Shortcake, and Mr. Kelly
The life and times of a mysterious patron at a rough and
ready 10th Avenue diner. 147

Chapter 31

$50 Prada Handbag
Where and how to buy the finest luxury brand knockoffs in
New York. 159

Chapter 32

Village Magic
Massive snowstorm makes time stand still in the West
Village. 163

Chapter 33

Raging Bull's Eight Wives
The former Middleweight Champion of the World explains
his marriage philosophy. 167

Chapter 34

Mel Brook's Place
Mel Brooks buys our seven-figure apartment for his son
with a memorable cast of professionals. 173

Chapter 35

Billie Holiday is Alive and Well
A lifelong New York couple says goodbye to their city
roots. 179

Chapter 36

Thirty-One Years Ago
An advertising legend and a former employee meet one last
time. 183

Chapter 1

Uncle Tip-Top
and Tony 4

JUNE 1952

Thanksgiving was a big deal in my family.

And Italian-American Thanksgiving dinner usually started about 1 PM. There was a giant antipasto course with cold cuts, olives, caponata, cheeses, marinated artichoke hearts and roasted peppers in olive oil, and enough Italian bread to feed a small city. The men usually washed down the food with a few gallons of cheap red wine. Then everybody took a ten-minute break before the lasagna course. Everybody was served at least a one-pound piece, and of course, there were meatballs, sausage, and spareribs cooked in a thin, red, Italian sauce for hours.

The prelims out of the way, it was now time for the "Indian stuff," as my Uncle Lou would say. Since my father was a wholesale butcher, he always seemed to be able to find a 30-plus-pound turkey. My Aunt Nellie, who was married to my father's brother, would always prepare the stuffing mix loaded with ground sausage, pinole nuts, milk-soaked bread, and a bunch of other olive-oil-soaked vegetables like mushrooms, zucchini, and peppers. Aunt Nellie was a worry-wart, so she always made an extra five to eight pounds of stuffing so that we wouldn't run short.

There were also the expected mashed potatoes: mashed, sweet with marshmallows, baked, and fried. At about 5 or 6 o'clock, there were still three courses to go: the after-dinner salad, the dessert tray, and the fruit, nut, and cheese course with finocchio (a stringent type of Italian celery).

In my house, the post-dinner break consisted of either an Italian digestive like Cynar (artichoke liqueur) or a glass of effervescent Brioschi (lemon-flavored baking soda). Both served the same purpose; make you belch and pass gas, to make room for the rest of the meal.

~

The family characters around the table were as interesting as the food. My recollection of Thanksgiving in 1952 has stuck with me for more than 60 years. Before the dessert course, my father's brothers Tom and Tony were discussing a business problem; in an Italian family like mine, everybody had a nickname. My father, who liked to sit backward in the chair when he ate was called "Jockey."

Uncle Tom supervised some 120 delivery trucks for the Ward Baking Company in the South Bronx. Their main product was Tip-Top bread that was delivered fresh daily to hundreds or area retailers. So, Uncle Tom was known as Uncle Tip-Top. In addition to his booming voice, I remember when he hugged you his facial stubble was so coarse, it felt like somebody was rubbing sandpaper across your cheek.

My father's other brother Tony was a butcher, who worked for my Dad in between doing "other things." His favorite phrase was "ahh go on." We never discussed what the "other things" were. All I know is one night Uncle Tony was bleeding petty badly, and my father took him to the emergency room. When the doctors finished, Uncle Tony wound up with four fingers on his left hand. I decided to call him Tony 4, just not to his face.

~

This particular Thanksgiving Uncle Tip-Top wanted his brother's advice on a personnel problem. For the past 15 years, my uncle had built a robust numbers racket using his drivers and the company trucks. Each driver was responsible for making so many stops; the store personnel placed bets through that delivery agent, and, if they won, the same delivery guy handled the payoffs. The delivery guy got a commission for every dollar bet, and, a bonus if one of his customers was a winner. The operation ran smoothly and never interfered with the timeliness of the bread deliveries. So everybody was happy.

Uncle Tip-Top had a trusted right-hand lieutenant, Angelo Sabatini, who made sure the numbers business run like clockwork. Angelo had made enough money in his side job to retire to Miami Beach and live a nice lifestyle. That left an opening. One of Tip-Top's senior drivers, Joe Jones, a black guy, got wind of Joe's retirement. He approached Tip-Top for the job. His pitch was that he had seniority (which he did), he knew the numbers business backward and forward (which he did) and was well-respected by all the customers, black and white (which he was).

Tony 4's eyes bulged out of his head. "You telling me you want to put a mulenyon (disparaging slang: black eggplant) in Sabatini's spot. You must be crazy. Next thing you know, he'll want to hire more mulenyons. And, before you know it they'll be mulenyons everywhere. Shit, Tip-Top is white bread!"

Jockey chimed in, "Gotta agree with Tony. Brothers don't lie."

Tip-Top raised a related issue. "Okay, suppose I pick someone with less time and grade like Mickey O'Hara, and Jones wants to file a complaint with the union."

Tony 4 paused. "You sayin' whack 'em?"

"I'm just saying, it would be a big problem," said Tip-Top.

"Then how about we just give him a non-management taste of the action," smiled Tony.

Tip-Top liked the idea but had another issue. "You mean I gotta keep books? Ain't never done that for anyone."

"What books," smiled Tony. "We give him what we give him."

"Suppose he wants to see how we got to that number?"

"Suppose he just disappears."

The three men started to laugh. Uncle Tip-Top grabbed his chest, his eyes rolled to the top of his head, and he fell head first in the huge platter of fruit, nuts, cheese and finocchio.

Chapter 2

Billy, Whitey, the Mick, and Me

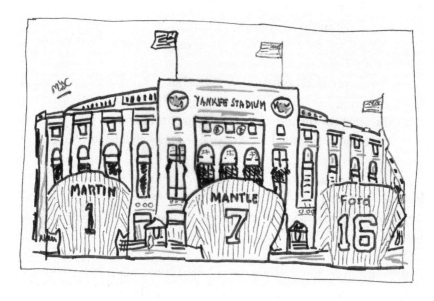

JULY 1955

As a kid growing up in the Bronx during the 1950s there was only one major baseball team in the world: the New York Yankees.

So, when Mom and Dad decided to send me to high school at All Hallows, an Irish Christian Brothers school on East 164th Street and Walton Avenue, just five blocks from Yankee Stadium, I was excited.

When my freshmen homeroom teacher Brother Powers told me the Stadium had called the school, looking for reliable young men who wanted to be part-time vendors at Yankee games, I was down at the Stadium Operations Office in a shot.

My interviewer, Timothy O'Toole, was a crusty, twinkle-eyed Irishman, who's red button nose suggested he'd had a drink or two in his lifetime.

"Kid," he stared, "How old are you?"

"Fourteen, sir."

"We like 'em a little older. You know this is the way it works — the newest guys have to carry those drink tanks up and down the upper deck. The longer you work, the lower the deck, and then you graduate to the real money: hot dogs, candy cotton, and, when you're 18, beer."

"Yes sir, I can do it," I replied confidently.

"You also gotta do Giants football in the winter."

"Yes sir, I can do it."

O'Toole sat back and smiled. "Brother Powers said you were a feisty one. He said, you were such a diehard Yankee fan, you'll clean the washrooms in order to hang around here."

The thought sounded revolting, but I was consistent. "Yes sir, I can do it."

"Kid, that was a joke! Vendors sell. Let's check the vocal cords. Imagine you're in the third deck, give me a shut."

I yelled at the top of my lungs, "Cold Soda, here! Get your cold soda here!"

O'Toole laughed. "Kid, you got the job. You need to show up at the employee gate at least two hours before game time. You get checked in and assigned a tank and an area. Then fill her up, and you're free to sell when you see customers. You get 20 percent of everything you sell."

"How do you know what I sell?"

"Simple, we count cups. You get 80 cups per tank. At 20 cents a cup, the tank is worth 16 bucks. You get more than three bucks a tank, and there is no limit to the number of tanks you can sell. You have to finish by the eighth inning so that the staff can clean the equipment for the next game."

~

I was now a working stiff. I checked the Yankee schedule and circled all the games I could attend. Most were on the weekend. There were also a few school holidays.

That first weekend — a Saturday day game and a Sunday doubleheader against the Boston Red Sox — I sold 33 tanks of drinks. I remember proudly showing my father the little brown envelope of $20 bills.

In the succeeding weeks I learned two other important things:

There was a way to make additional income per tank. All you had to do was take 8 to 10 good looking cups out of the trash. Clean and dry them. Put them back in the slot, return to the vendor shack, and explain you were "shorted on liquid." The dispatcher would add some liquid, and you'd go out and sell the stuff, before receiving the next full tank. At 20 cents a cup, my tank yield about five dollars instead of three, an increase of over 60 percent. In the process, I also learned: don't get greedy, you only do the short once a day for single games, twice for doubleheaders.

~

The second thing I learned was that the employee gate opened four hours before game time. You were free to watch Yankee batting and fielding practice from the box seats right behind the Yankee dugout. If you were lucky enough, you could ask for autographs from anyone willing to sign.

~

I'll never forget that first practice session. I was walking through the tunnel in my Yankee cap and vendor tag on the way to the box seats. Walking directly toward me were Phil Rizzuto and Yogi Berra. I froze in my tracks. They couldn't have been nicer. "Hey kid, today it's hot dogs, maybe tomorrow you're behind home plate. Yogi can't do this forever." They patted me on the back and continued on their way.

That summer, I must have worked every weekend game and was always one of the first to arrive so I could sit in the first row.

The voice of the Yankees, Mel Allen, usually arrived first — with a hangover. As he passed, he'd tip his cap, as he stumbled upstairs to the broadcast booth. "Hey kid, happy day," he'd say in his Southern drawl. I would smile and nod back.

One day, Mel walked over to the stands and waved me over, "What's your name, Kid?"

"Matt," I responded.

Mel whispered, "Tomorrow, Kid, tomorrow, Kid." I had no idea what he was talking about, but Sunday morning I made extra sure, I was the first employee in line at the gate.

After grabbing my hat and badge, I hustled to the seat to the right of the dugout. I was so close to the field, I could touch the grass. A number of the Yankees made their way out of the dugout, including Hank Bauer, Elston Howard, the Scooter, and Yogi.

~

About a half hour later, Mel stumbled out of the Yankee bullpen in right field, followed by three equally wobbly Yankees, laughing and yuckin' it up — Billy Martin, Eddy Lopat, and Mickey Mantle.

The four of them walked over to me. Mel smiled. "Fellas, I want ya' ll to meet my friend Matt. He's here every day. He loves you guys." Whitey took a ball out of his pocket. He looked at the Mick, "Think you got enough to sign it."

Mickey smiled and took the pen; his hand was shaking as he tried to sign the ball. The ball slid out of the Mick's hands; Billy snared it before it hit the ground. "You kids from Oklahoma gotta learn to hold your booze better," laughed Billy.

After a little more verbal banter, the three of them scribbled their signatures, and Billy flipped me the ball.

As they left, I was surrounded by the other vendors, speechless at what they had just witnessed.

~

Deliriously happy, I went upstairs to get my tank. I hid the ball in my street clothing and tucked it in the back of the personal effects shelf. When the game was over, I returned to gather my treasure. The ball was gone.

So here I am more than 50 years later, still smarting, with just the memory of Billy, Whitey, the Mick, and me.

Chapter 3

Marvin,
Where are You?

DECEMBER 1957

Growing up, I guess my family was closet racists.

When I helped my father at the wholesale markets, I never saw a black employee. At gatherings of family and friends I never saw a black person. When my uncles told their stories of life, never once did they mention a black person. So growing up, it was not surprising I didn't have one black friend.

We lived in a rough, melting-pot section of the Bronx called Fort Apache. It began around 138th Street and ended at about 153rd Street. As a lifelong resident, you just learned what street to walk down, and tried to get in before dark. My father's advice was always the same. "Stay away from the black kids, you just never know."

Home was a relatively undistinguished apartment building on 149th Street, populated by Jews, Mics, and Wops. There wasn't a person of color, any color, in the 66 apartments. My best friends were Georgie Fenner (a Jew), Franklin Donato (a Wop), and Carl O'Donnell (a Mic). Not one of them was the least athletic. Georgie, the intellectual, read books and complained about his deviated septum; Franklin loved his black leather jacket and stealing cigarettes from the Marino's Grocery Mart; and goofy, gangly Carl saw the world as half empty, all the time.

~

One day at Sunday Mass, our parish priest, Father George, mentioned St. Anselm's was going to have tryouts for the new under-18 CYO (Catholic Youth Organization) basketball team, I said why not, after all, I had been one of the best players on my high school intramural team.

St. Anselm's was a pretty poor parish, and the gymnasium reflected that fact. The basketball court was the conventional length. But the baskets were bolted to the brick walls at the end of the room. In other words, the distance between the end line and the wall was about six inches. So anytime you mixed it up under the basket, there was the distinct possibility somebody would try to ram your head into the wall.

The court had two other unique features. The width was about half regulation size, so playing a five-on-five basketball game was like standing in a crowded subway train. Also, there were no courtside seats. Spectators, if any, stood on a side balcony that overlooked the court.

Tryouts were interesting. I noticed I was the only white kid! When we scrimmaged, I couldn't help but notice; nobody wanted to pass the ball to me. When I did get it, I would toss up an outside shot rather than mix it up around the basket.

As luck (and a bit of skill) would have it, my "A" game showed up for the scrimmage. I made my first five outside shots in a row. The biggest stud on the court, Marvin, about six-foot-three-inches and 240 pounds, noticed. On one sequence, he grabbed the rebound, waved at me, then threw a football pass the length of the court, which allowed me to make an easy lay-up.

One of the other guys got in Marvin's face, "What you doin' that for, man?"

Marvin replied simply, "I want to win."

I made the team. The coach, Father Francis — the only black priest I had ever met — decided to make me the starting point guard. In basketball lingo that means the person generally assigned to dribbling the ball up the court and setting up plays for the rest of the team.

The second biggest player on the team, J-Rock, complained, "Father, this ain't gonna work when we go the 125th Street Y." The rest of the team nodded their heads. I had no idea what the comment was all about.

Father replied, "J-Rock, why don't you leave that up to God and me."

We had our first official league game at the YMCA on 125th Street near Tenth Avenue. As we warmed up, I looked around. I was the only white player on either team, and everybody in the stands was black. The whistle blew. Marvin tapped the ball to me. I started dribbling down the court. Somebody yelled from the stands, "Honkey with the ball, honkey with the ball." Marvin got behind the distracted players. I tossed him the ball for an easy layup.

J-Rock and Marvin grabbed the majority of the rebounds and scored most of our points during the first half. We were winning, 29 to 12. With two seconds left, I dribbled the ball up the court and tossed it to Marvin, again. This time three guys climbed all over him leaving me unguarded at the foul line. Marvin passed the ball to me. Swish. The buzzer went off; the half was over. Two black guys ran on the court and got in my face. "Get off *our* court, Honkey."

Marvin stomped over and pushed both of them into the stands. The place turned silent. I was thinking all hell was about to break loose. Instead, one of the parents walked out on the court, and said "Boys, good first half. Can't wait for the second."

Marvin and I played just that one season together. I haven't seen him in more than 50 years.

~

Fast forward thirty-three years to 1980. My son Mark had just tried out for the high school basketball team. He walked in with a big smile on his face.

"How'd you do?"

"I made the team, Dad."

I gave him a big hug.

"And I made a new friend, J.L." Mark waved to the doorway. A shy, little black kid entered, cautiously.

"J.L., welcome. Always nice to meet a friend of Mark's."

Unlike Marvin and me, J.L. and Mark became lifelong friends. Mark is the godfather to J.L.'s son Zake, and J.L. was the first usher in Mark's wedding party. And despite the fact they now live on different coasts, 3,000 miles apart, they talk at least once a week and visit each other in person at least once a year.

Makes me wonder, Marvin, where are you?

Chapter 4

Y.A. Tittle's
Hot Chocolate

NOVEMBER 1961

I was a 20-years-old college junior and one of the senior vendors at Yankee Stadium.

During the summer, I graduated from selling soft drinks at 14 years old to hotdogs at 16 and beer at 18 (remember this was 1961) and had the privilege of watching Mickey Mantle and Whitey Ford become superstars. I would sell product for six innings, then find a free seat, before returning to the vendor stand to check out. By definition, I was usually the last to check in; the managers never once complained. They knew we were good kids who wanted to earn spending money and have fun doing it!

During the winter, Yankee Stadium was the place to sell hot chocolate and hotdogs during the New York Football Giant games, and watch them grind out win after win on the backs of Hall-of-Famers Charlie Conerly, Frank Gifford, Alex Webster, Sam Huff, and Andy Robustelli. Usually, I'd sell until midway in the third quarter, then find a seat somewhere out of view. Like in the summer, I was usually the last to check in.

The fall 1961 edition of the Giants was going to be different. Conerly, Gifford, and Webster were gone; the offense was depleted. In August, the Giants made two controversial trades. They got an aging 34-year-old bald quarterback from the San Franciso 49ers, Y.A. Tittle, and the injury-prone, sure-handed receiver, Del Shofner, from the Los Angeles Rams.

Nobody, including yours truly, knew what to expect. Most New Yorkers didn't believe a candy-soft Californian would survive with a grind 'em-out team built for New York's windy winters. It turned out we were all wrong. By the fourth game of the season, they became the league's most exciting offensive duo and would remain that way until the mid-60's.

~

During the winter of '61, I also learned something else: it was far more profitable to sell ticket holders in the upper deck hot chocolate. Two reasons: every seat was sold out, and the biting wind usually left them panting for something hot. The Harry M. Stevens coffee sucked, so that left hot chocolate. The only issue was that a full tank of 80 cups strapped to your back was like adding 30 pounds, and you had to walk up and down some pretty steep steps. But New Yorkers learn to deal with workarounds. Every time I got tired, I'd rest the tank on the railing just above the lower boxes. What made the spot ideal was the fact that I didn't block anybody's view. The box seat patrons were below me, and the grandstand level started a few feet above my vendor cap.

~

Sunday, November 21. It was bitter cold. Maybe 15 degrees with winds gusts of 20 to 30 miles an hour. The San Francisco Forty-Niners were in town for a rare appearance. The crowd was buying hot chocolate like there was no tomorrow. I was exhausted from running up and down, back and forth. A little after halftime, I had already made twice what I usually made during an entire game.

The game was an offensive feast with both teams going up and down the field, so I decided to take a break and watch the game. I balanced the tank on the rail at the top of the box seats directly below me. Shofner caught a long Tittle pass and headed for the end zone. I jumped up and down and start cheering. I looked at the scoreboard; we're already halfway through the third quarter. I decided when this tanks empty, I'm done for the day.

The crisp air was filled with the smell of hot chocolate and clouds of white steam. Suddenly, I heard a scream, "What the fuck." I looked down. The guy sitting below me in a checkered wool topcoat is drenched in hot chocolate. I notice the tank lever wedged under the bar, and the liquid was pouring out at a prodigious pace. He started up the steps after me waving his arms. He's huge... "You stupid son of a bitch, I'll have your..."

I didn't wait to find out what he'll have. I took off and ran all the way to the end of the top deck and hid in the last stall of the bathroom. I didn't make a sound till I was absolutely positively sure the game was over and the place quiet as a church.

~

About ninety minutes later, I heard the janitors cleaning the floor and urinals. I came out of the stall like nothing ever happened and walked back to the vendor station. If my manager Bill was gone, I'd leave the tank outside the kitchen area, and assume somebody will be by in the morning. Best case, Bill was still there, and I'd collect my earnings and get the hell out of there.

To my surprise, when I arrived, not only was Bill still there but so was the guy in the chocolate flavored topcoat. Bill said, "Say hello to Mr. DeAngelis. I think you owe him something."

The guy glared down at me. I was frightened to death. He broke into a broad smile. "Kid, I've never seen anybody run so fast with a tank of chocolate. Tell you what, pay for dry cleaning the coat and we'll call it even."

Bill also smiled at me. "Matt, there's more good news. You sold enough hot chocolate today to pay for the cleaning. There's even a buck ten left over."

Bill handed me a dollar and a dime.

Chapter 5

Wedding Night at The Plaza

NOVEMBER 1964

"I'm sorry sir, The Plaza does not have a wedding suite," said the voice on the other end of the phone, with a proper hint of condescending, snobbish sarcasm.

"You don't?" I responded naively. (After all, I was a thoroughly intimidated, 23-year-old, middle-class male from the Bronx, desperately seeking to establish a rapport with the assistant manager of the world-famous and super-pricey Plaza Hotel on 59th Street.

"No, Sir," sighed the increasingly impatient voice. "Our suite accommodations range from a modest, but pleasant junior suite to a most luxurious suite-and-three."

I hadn't the foggiest notion what to say, so I went to my last resort strategy — blow smoke! "Sir, it's my wedding night, sir. As I worked my way through Yale (never happened), my fiancée Mary Ann, would rave about her family's periodic weekend sojourns to New York City and the Plaza Hotel (never happened), so I decided I'd surprise her. What would you suggest?"

"Oh, how very romantic, sir. Now I understand better," said a suddenly warmer assistant blowing his own smoke. "The Suite and Three is the appropriate choice for such an auspicious occasion. I assure you, Mr. Crisci, Mary Ann will be impressed with your sensitivity and exquisite taste. I'll make a notation on the reservation that it's your Wedding Night. The Plaza will do everything possible to make it a night filled with memories she will cherish forever. Been married thirty years myself, remember our Wedding Night vividly. Too bad I didn't think of the Plaza back then. Ahhh, the glorious ignorance of youth. Right, sir?"

~

I attempted to impersonate a 30-year-old, the son of a wealthy, pretentious upper-class snob, "Quite so, quite so, my good man."

"By the way sir, my name is Roger. How would you like to guarantee the room?"

Without a moment's hesitation, I mumbled, "American Express." *Thank goodness my first credit card had arrived two days earlier!*

After I hung up, I realize I had never asked the cost of a Suite and Three. I post-rationalized, with 200 middle-class wedding guests, we should certainly collect at least $5,000 in cash (The Italian wedding custom was hard cash only). So, worst case — a bizarre room rate of say $500 plus taxes — there'd still be plenty left over for a down payment on a new car we both wanted.

~

Two days before the big event, Mary Ann chided sweetly, "Honey, shouldn't we be thinking about where we to stay on our Wedding Night? Remember, we have an 8 AM flight to Jamaica."

Proud as a peacock, I announced, "It's all taken care of, Babe (author's note: a politically acceptable, non-sexist sign of affection used by middle-class Italian families), we're staying at The Plaza Hotel."

My bride's face beamed. "Honey (then a politically acceptable non-sexist sign of affection used by middle-class Italian families), you certainly know how to treat your lady."

~

The wedding ceremony and reception came and went. The in-laws invited all their friends and spent a ton — live band, cocktail party, fabulous dinner, and a desert buffet. We met at least 100 people we didn't know and posed for at least 200 family pictures. And the guests stuffed Mary Ann's white silk purse with cards and envelopes containing twenty and fifty-dollar bills.

While the party was still in full swing, we agreed it was time to bid adieu; after all, we had more important matters to consummate on this evening.

We arrived at The Plaza around midnight with enough bags to suggest we were embarking on vacation for the entire Winter Season. Upon entering the Plaza, I was flabbergasted. The lobby looked like the Palace of Versailles: marble floors, arched gold leaf ceilings, crystal chandeliers, and twenty-foot palm trees in the lobby. Despite this intimidating opulence, the check-in process was warm and efficient. Everybody made a fuss over us. Roger obviously had made the "just married" notation prominent as hell because the entire staff seemed to know.

A tall, thin, articulate bellhop named Burton, actually a Shakespearean actor between gigs led us to *our room*. The elevator opened on the 20th floor. The bellhop motioned as if waving a giant medieval sword, "To the right, down the end of the hall." Two enormous mahogany doors swung open, "Welcome, Mr. and Mrs. Crisci, to the Plaza's finest."

The entrance hall was larger than the living room in our apartment, and it was decorated to the hilt. Five-foot-wide crystal chandelier, Chippendale settee, golden brown marble floor and a spectacular bouquet of fresh Casablanca lilies on the circular Queen Anne table. My thoughts ran the gamut from *Wow, gorgeous! To Good Christ! What the hell have I done?*

Mary Ann sighed in delight, "Babe, I adore you."

As we were about to discover, we hadn't seen anything yet!

The tour began modestly enough. "This is your living room, sir, over there, your dining room and kitchen, and a guest bathroom. A bit further down the hall, your library, the guest bedroom with adjoining bath." Burton then proudly opened two ten-foot high carved doors, "And this is your master suite and private bath equipped with Jacuzzi, steam bath and sauna."

The apartment, the home, the whatever, was a mini-replica of one of those sixteenth-century French palaces featured in Architectural Digest. Louie the Fourteenth furniture everywhere, plus four televisions and five phones. Once the selected luggage was unpacked, Burton discretely vaporized.

"This place is drop-dead," said my new wife. "I'm afraid to ask, but how much did all this cost?"

I decided to blow smoke. "Forget the money; this is our Wedding Night. I wanted it to be something we'd always remember."

~

Time to settle in for a "romantic" late night rendezvous. As we sat in the ballroom-size living room, I could sense Mary Ann's nervousness. I placed my arm around her neck and shoulder. Goosebumps formed on her arms and legs. "Hey, honey," I whispered reassuringly, "why don't we order a few drinks — I have to be honest with you, I'm a little nervous."

Mary Ann breathed a sigh of relief, like a convict on death row who had been granted an extension seconds before that fateful moment, "Extra dry Martini," she blurted. "Make it a double."

"Sounds good to me, think I'll order the same."

I called room service. A friendly voice took the order, "Very good, Mr. Crisci, would you like them shaken or stirred? I thought to myself, thank goodness for the James Bond movies. "Generally, I prefer them shaken, at The Plaza I prefer them stirred."

The voice said, "Understand sir. Your drinks will be right up." Five minutes later, shoes removed, the stereo playing some sultry Barbara Streisand, there was a knock at the door. "Room service, sir." In strolled a beautiful silver-serving cart with a huge basket of fruits, cheeses, nuts, and, *a liter carafe* of dry Martinis! The waiter smiled, "The food basket is compliments of The Plaza, our little gift to the newlyweds."

"Why, thank you."

"Shall I pour the Martinis sir? We nodded yes. The waiter slowly filled two enormous V-shaped basins sitting on top of thin foot long crystal stems. I couldn't help but notice, even with the two glasses filled the carafe was only about a third empty. *Holy cow, we have enough Martinis for a night-long college frat party!* We toasted each other, then wolfed down the two Tini's like they were lemonade.

Mary Ann was now totally relaxed; the goosebumps were completely gone. *Ho, ho, ho, I* thought, *won't be long before we're in that gorgeous king-size bed.* I'd been dreaming of this moment since Mary Ann announced six months ago in the heat of passion, "this is the last real sex until we're married." I was horny as hell.

Unknowingly, I made *the* fatal mistake. "Another Martini?"

~

The second Tini's were quickly consumed; a certain giddiness appeared. "Looks like one more each and the carafe will be history," I smiled. "You know Scott and Zelda Fitzgerald used to drink Martinis when they stayed at the Plaza. Then they'd walk across the street and dance around the great fountain. Scott thought it enhanced their love life."

Feeling absolutely no pain, I continued, "How about we skip the fountain idea and head straight to bed?"

"Agreed," she said.

~

We struggled to get out from the deep, plush couch. Mary Ann stumbled backward, laughing.

Another knock at the door. I mumbled, *"This better be God damn important!"* There stood our smiling, courteous Plaza waiter, "Sir, sorry to bother you, but we forgot to bring this earlier. Compliments of Roger." There, on the sterling silver cart, sat a chilled magnum of Dom Perignon in a bucket of ice with two beautiful fluted champagne glasses. "You must be an important somebody; the '59 Dom was an exceptional vintage. Shall I open it?"

Mary Ann smiled and said, "Your move, Stud."

I looked at the empty martini carafe, "Sure, what the hell." The popped cork flew some 40 feet into the adjoining study. The waiter retrieved the cork from under the couch by crawling on all fours. We laughed at the huge butt dressed in black pants. After what seemed like an eternity, the waiter left with the cork in hand.

A warm caress, a juicy kiss, a tender tug at her undergarments, and then a glass of Dom. And then another glass of Dom, and another. Mary Ann suddenly became a human vacuum cleaner, shamelessly sucking the stuff up. Somehow, someway, we finished the entire magnum; we were totally sloshed.

~

We made it to the master bedroom by using the walls for support. It was like walking down the aisle of an airplane after being struck by a sudden patch of turbulence. I struggled to remove the bedspread from the huge king-size bed. It felt like I was single-handedly removing the infield tarp at Yankee Stadium after a long, soggy rain delay. Mary Ann clung desperately to the red satin curtain by the window.

(The ensuing events, regarding sex are still very sketchy at best. I *think we made love* and Mary Ann *thinks* we consummated our marriage –but frankly, neither of us can swear to it.) But the remainder of the evening had a distinct clarity. I started to dizzily fade into dreamland as the room went round and round. Mary Ann rolled over and cuddled in my arms. Suddenly, weird sounds similar to jungle mating calls emanated from her mouth as she slowly and somewhat ungracefully slid over to the edge of the bed. Her head slowly rose like a mystical ancient god in *Raiders of the Lost Ark,* then slumped forward as a stream of thick, creamy, multi-textured liquid tumbled to the floor near her side of the bed. *Christ, what a mess!*

"Babe, so, so sorry, just couldn't help it," she said sweetly, as bumpy little white particles sat on her lips. Like a volcano close to full eruption, selected bits continuously dribbled out of her mouth onto the silk sheets. Moments later, a horrifying, "Oh God there's more. Got to get to the bathroom before I ...." I then watched Mary Ann's well-proportioned, naked body, ricochet off the walls like a cue ball in bumper pool as she made her way to the bathroom.

While she was making grotesque sounds in the distance, I gathered myself, stripped the bed of soiled, soggy sheets, pillows, and blankets, stumbled into the guest bedroom, removed the clean sheets and linens, and placed them on the bed in the master suite. *Sure, glad I had the foresight to reserve a suite with an extra bed and linens*, I thought to myself.

Eventually, the squeals and moans subsided in the bathroom. I called out, "Do you need some help?"

"No, I'm fine now," mumbled a low, unsure voice, and Lady Love crashed into the center of the nice clean bed and snuggled under a big down Plaza Hotel comforter. I wedged into a narrow strip of real estate on the other side of the bed.

About 4 AM, I noticed *my* side of the bed was soaked in gooey, sticky liquid; I bounced out of bed like a pogo stick. Mary Ann stirred, "Love you, honey," she mumbled. "Sorry about the mess. Come sleep by my side.... Always." She faded back to dreamland. "Don't worry dear," I whispered to the smelly, snoring corpse.

~

Morning arrived, about two and a half hours later, like nothing ever happened. As the waiter wheeled in a sumptuous breakfast, he couldn't help but notice the magnum of Dom and the empty Martini carafe.

"Looks you and your guests had a good evening," he said with a smile. "Shall I take this away?"

"Yes, it was a good evening" I replied.

As I signed the breakfast bill, I noticed the tab was almost $150, not including gratuity. *If breakfast was $150, God only knows how much the damn Suite and Three cost!*

I was desperate for the answer but didn't want to embarrass myself in front of my new bride. "Babe, why don't you and the Bellman take care of the bags? I'll settle the bill. Meet you in the lobby by the main door.

"Good idea," she said. "What about the wedding gifts?"

"The wedding gifts?"

"The money, the $4,900 we collected."

"Oh, I'll take it. We can get Traveler's Checks at the airport."

~

"Good morning Mr. Crisci," said a cheery face at the front desk. "Was everything satisfactory?"

I smiled and nodded.

"How will you be settling the bill?" The hand passed a paper across the marble counter. I knew this moment not going to be the highlight of the Wedding Night. The total was $4,790. I shit in my pants! The guy behind the counter noticed my surprise.

"I'm so glad you noticed, Mr. Crisci. Roger asked us to take 20 percent off the bill, a little wedding gift from The Plaza, hope you don't mind?"

"Thank you very much. The Plaza made last night an extraordinary occasion." I then passed my new American Express Card across the counter. I thought to myself, *at least I still l have the bag of cash.*

~

Fifty-four years later, we are still happily married, have three wonderful sons and two amazing grandchildren. And, neither Mary Ann or I have had an extra dry, double martini since our wedding night at The Plaza.

Chapter 6

Buitoni Spaghetti and Abbie Hoffman

MARCH 1969

They say the leaf doesn't fall far from the tree. I'm not sure who "they" is, but in the case of my mother and I that was true.

When Mom was 51, she had to go back to work for the first time in 26 years because my dad went broke in business. Actually, he did more than go broke, he died in his sleep at age 60, owing the IRS two million in bad taxes and penalties.

But, you gotta hand it to Mom, she took the blows and kept ticking. She somehow convinced a New York Telephone Company supervisor, Helen Conway, she could be a great telephone operator because she was a great talker. Helen patiently watched Mom struggle inserting and removing the cables on the operator's switchboard until she learned how to do the job.

~

Mom then worked evenings shift for the next 14 years because it paid more money. She took two buses to work, and never missed a day, regardless of the weather. When she retired she had a pension, some AT&T stock, and free medical, dental insurance and telephone service for life. Between those assets and her social security, she lived a comfortable lower-middle-class life. Mom died peacefully surrounded by family at the age of 93.

Before I spoke at the funeral, I did a calculation. During Mom's 14 years at New York Telephone, she earned $112,000. During her 28 years in retirement, she received about $241,000 in pension payouts and free telephone calls. My hypochondriac Mom also spent significant sums of company money on an endless array of doctors and dentists.

~

During retirement, Mom discovered new ways to stretch her income. It all started with a box of Buitoni Brand spaghetti. Mom had made her tomato sauce and was about to put the spaghetti into the boiling water. She noticed a tiny dead brown bug in the box. Since the Buitoni Brand had walked on water in our household for years, she used her free long-distance telephone service to track down the president's name and address in Italy. She wrote a hand-written letter explaining her disappointment in production quality control. To her, and my, amazement, the company not only sent a letter of apology, but they also mailed a case of 24 boxes of spaghetti.

A lightbulb went off in her head. She wondered if she complained to other food manufacturers, would she get the same response? Next up was JELL-O — the same result; then Post cereals — more boxes. When Mom died, her cabinets were filled with a large variety of packaged foods she never had time to prepare or the appetite to eat.

~

Fast forward to me. It was the wild and wholly 60's. I was smitten with the societal inequities between the haves and have-nots, long before Bernie Sanders.

Eldridge Cleaver, Jerry Rubin, Huey P. Newton, and Abbie Hoffman become my aspirational role models, despite my professed desire to climb the corporate ladder of power and wealth.

Abbie, a kid from Brooklyn, wrote a book called *Steal This Book*. The concept was simple; the book contained ways to game the system. As an example, he challenged readers not to buy the book but to steal it instead, preferably from store bookshelves, and, if necessary from friends and neighbors. Abbie made an entire generation believe that *intelligent theft* was its social statement. While I'm not sure I bought Abbie's entire premise, I found Abbie gaming strategy aspirationally attractive. It reminded me of mom.

~

At this point, I had talked my way into the lowest level job that existed at the prestigious Young and Rubicam Advertising Agency on Madison Avenue — traffic department, where I was paid $68 a week (pre-tax). I was determined to show the powers that be a kid from the South Bronx with a degree from a local commuter college could compete successfully with the elite MBA's from Harvard, Yale, and Wharton.

Mary Ann knew Y&R was my dream. She also knew $68 a week couldn't support a wife, a kid, and another on the way. So, she went to work part-time to make ends meet. As for me, I knew my meager salary wouldn't allow the luxury of lunch at a midtown diner or sandwich shop.

Abbie Hoffman's book flashed in my mind. I thought to myself *what would Abbie do in my situation?* The answer came on the 7th Avenue IRT to the Bronx! I would start each day with a substantial breakfast that would tide me over until dinner. Abbie devoted an entire chapter as to "how" in his book. But the plan required an accomplice. Fortunately, most of my traffic department peers suffered similar financial constraints. So I convinced one of them, a guy named Bubba Sutton from Georgia, to join my breakfast club.

Here's how it worked. New York was a city of cluttered, noisy, busy diners with Formica counters and stainless steel stools waiting to be gamed. As per Abbie, Bubba entered the targeted diner first, sat on a stool and ordered a complete breakfast with his distinctive southern drawl. I waited outside for him to signal when the stool next to him was empty. He wolfed down his eggs over medium, a double order of sausages, home-fried potatoes, rye toast, and coffee, then asked for the check. I ordered a cup of coffee and an English muffin and asked for my check. Then we'd switch checks, and Bubba would go to the cashier at the door and pay for coffee and muffin.

I waited until he was completely out of sight, then courteously pointed out the error to the waitress, "Madame, there must be some mistake. I just had coffee and a muffin." She'd apologize. Sometimes, I paid for the coffee and muffin. However, most of the time the diner manager was so embarrassed they never charged me.

Bubba and I would then walk a to another diner blocks away, and reverse the process. Before we started our day, we both had a nice full stomach.

~

I don't remember how many times Bubba and I had breakfast together, but my recollection was that Manhattan was home to more than 270 Abbie Hoffman diners. In time, I was promoted into account management replete with an expense account, which put my gaming-the-system days to rest.

As for Bubba, he never got promoted, and left Y&R in a huff.

Chapter 7

World-Famous Baloney Omelets

MAY 1971

One of the greatest contributions to the New York culinary landscape is the genuine, All-American Jewish delicatessen.

Not the tourist traps like the Carnegie Deli on Seventh Avenue where a four-inch high, pastrami and corned beef "Woody" on rye cost $29.99. No wonder the place finally closed down in 2016! My preference was places like Berger's Deli on 47th between Fifth and Sixth where Howie Berger's family served corned-beef and pastrami and chopped liver at half the price of its well-publicized competitors for 50 years.

~

Originally, I stumbled on the unassuming place by accident one morning in 1971. I spotted the yellow and red canvas awning above a narrow storefront with a few delivery bikes in front. The awning read simply: "Berger's. Since 1956. Great food. Good prices." Promising.

I looked inside. Berger's was long, narrow, and undistinguished. On the left, a few feet from the entrance, was a huge refrigerated cabinet filled with meats, cheeses, and smoked fish. The sign above said, "take out." Next to the refrigerated cabinet was a cash register, which made it impossible to leave without paying your bill.

Beyond the cabinet was a Formica counter with 20 stools. They looked directly at the short-order cook in front of a massive grill. On the other side of the room, they had somehow squeezed two rows of Formica tables, leaving the waitress and patrons about 18 inches to walk between the tables and the counter. The place was noisy, crowded, frenetic, and smelled great. I picked up the menu. The damn thing was about eight laminated pages of well-priced options. I liked the vibe and decided to stay.

~

I stood near the doorway and waited for an open stool. A feisty little waitress with long curly brown hair and a thick Spanish accent got in my face, "Don't block the door. Got regulars. Want a spinner?" I nodded. She pointed, "over there between Moishe and Morris."

I squeezed between two husky men talking to each other. I offered to switch seats. Morris said, "Never sit next to Moishe. He's a thief. He specializes in stealing diamonds from wholesalers trying to make a fair profit." Moishe responded. "Fair profit. You're the thief." I thought to myself, *are these guys getting ready to rumble?*

Moishe saw concern written all over my face, "Kid, don't worry. The thief and I have been doing business for 20 years. All works out in the end."

Crisis averted. I went back to ordering breakfast. Rosie looked at me. "Watcha want?"

Morris whispered in my ear, "The bologna omelet with extra muenster (cheese). It's world-famous." I took Morris's advice. Rosie yelled my order to the cook with his back to me about two feet away. "Juan Diego, Howie special, extra muenster." The oriental short-order cook turned around, "Rosie, gotta stop with the extras, Howie gets mad."

"You wanna cook or wait on the customers?" she responded.

He turned around and started mumbling to himself in Japanese. Then he placed what appeared to be a quarter-pound stick of butter on the hot grill, added three freshly cracked eggs and two thick slices of bologna. As the eggs cooked, Juan Diego added slices of muenster cheese on top, then flipped the side to create a thick, gooey omelet. Rosie placed the massive dish in front of me; it was about 3,000 calories and deliciously decadent.

Morris cautioned, "Kid, careful. One too many will give you a heart attack!"

Moishe responded, "Ignore him, kid. Look at me, I'm 165 pounds, and eat two a week." Moishe interrupted. "Next time tell Rosie to add extra bologna cubes on top, you won't be sorry." The two men got their checks and left.

Rosie put her hand on her hips. "Millionaires. Cheapskates. What am I gonna do with twenty-five cents." Intimidated, I looked at my $5 check and decided to leave Rosie a two-dollar tip. She smiled. "Come back soon."

~

I walked over to the heavyset man at the cash register. A guy with thick stovepipe arms behind the refrigerated counter was arguing with the delivery boy. "Just deliver the stuff; what the hell do you care if they want chopped liver for breakfast, you ain't the doctor."

The man looked at Herbie, "Am I right or what, Herbie?"

Herbie laughed, then turned to me and said, "Everything okay. Haven't seen you before."

"That's about to change," I responded. "Best bologna omelet I ever had in my life." I became a Berger's baloney omelet regular for the next 35 years.

~

Sadly, Berger's Deli closed in late 2006. The last time I spoke to Howie, he was proud of the fact that his two sons graduated from Columbia with honors — compliments of the deli's generous cash flow. He also said, neither wanted anything to do with the business; they had other plans.

Chapter 8

Veal and Peas in Brown Gravy

JULY 1972

Life was good. I was climbing the ranks at Young & Rubicam and rapidly becoming a Manhattan restaurant aficionado thanks to my fun-loving clients and deft use of corporate expense accounts.

One evening over dinner, my wife told me a young Brazilian doctor, Luis Mattias, who worked with her at Misericordia Hospital in the Bronx, had decided to return to Rio with his wife, Tanya, to build his practice and raise a family. I suggested: we have a proper bon voyage celebration in Manhattan.

The swarthy Luis looked the part of a Latin movie matinee idol: wavy black hair, dark eyebrows, a well-maintained mustache, and heavy Latin accent. Tanya was equally striking with a flawless complexion, the high cheekbones of a fashion model, and a figure to match. Her plan on return to Brazil was to have at least three children and run 20+ mile marathons, which had become her passion during their five years in New York.

Since we had spent many evenings together, we knew the Mattias's were well-traveled, so Mary Ann and I decided the sendoff should have a European flair. I suggested an elegant French bistro on 51st Street and First Avenue called La Copain. The place had become quite popular since my first visit because it had been featured in the Academy Award film, "The French Connection," a year earlier.

Afterward, we agree to visit Tanya's family apartment on East 63rd, where her father, Joao — the U.S. President of the Bank of Brazil — spent significant time.

~

When we arrived at the restaurant, the place was bustling, but our reservation request for a corner table was honored. I knew Luis's English wasn't the best, so a quiet corner seemed reasonable.

A polished waiter dressed in a tuxedo and starched shirt handed me a wine list in an impressive red-leather folder. "La carte des vins, monsieur." I scanned the wine list and selected what appeared to be two reasonably-priced Bordeauxs. The waiter pursed his lips, "Êtes-vous sûr, monsieur?" Reluctantly, the snooty waiter opened the bottle, poured a taste in Luis's glass, placed the cork next to Luis, and waited. Luis waved his arm and said, "sí, sí."

Mary Ann and Luis recalled a few humorous professional moments at the hospital, as we consumed the first bottle. I motioned to our waiter to uncork the second bottle. Eyebrows raised, he unceremoniously dumped the entire bottle into our glasses. Impatiently, he asked "Voulez-vous commander un apéritif?"

Tanya, who spoke some French, said we aren't quite ready to order and that we'd like to see the wine list again. The waiter walked away in a huff; he wanted to turn the table as fast as possible. We consumed two more bottles of wine. We were soon laughing loudly and slurring our words. Luis's clipped English was now almost impossible to understand.

Spokesperson Tanya asked for the menus. She explained the options to Luis. He ordered an Oysters Rockefeller starter. Tanya moved to the entrées. She read the item in French and described it in Portuguese. Luis shook his head after each one as if to say, "okay, but what else?" We found the whole process hysterical. The waiter did not.

Finally, Tanya asked sweetly, "Are there any house specials? The waiter said something in French about veal scaloppini with fresh peas in our mint-flavored brown sauce. Tanya turned to Luis and tried to explain the offering in Portuguese, but there is no precise equivalent for the word scaloppini.

Luis made a face. "Eh?" She tried again. Luis stared quizzically, "Eh. Eh." I broke up. The infuriated waiter thought I was laughing at him. He looked at Luis and said with no accent, "It's veal and peas in brown gravy, got it mac?"

~

Dinner over, we stumbled out the door into a waiting cab, which stopped in front of a gorgeous high-rise with circular driveway on East 63rd not far from the East River. Moments later we were admiring the Manhattan skyline from an expansive top-floor apartment with 360- degree views.

The remainder of the evening followed Brazilian social customs. We laughed and drank bottles of rum and danced to the Latin beat until 5 AM. Exhausted, we all bedded down. I laid on the floor unable to reach the couch. Tanya smiled and said, "Lightweight, never survive in Rio."

Chapter 9

Footsteps on 47th

SEPTEMBER 1974

This story began six years before; I just didn't know it at the time.

I'd been at Young and Rubicam six years. A memo circulated about the company opening an office in Sydney, Australia. It was going to be run by a fellow by the name of Joe DeDeo. He was a Princeton graduate. But the scuttlebutt was he was more of a street fighter, who was always butting heads with other senior managers. The rumor was that sending him to Australia was a classy way of getting him out of New York.

I somehow talked his secretary into giving me 15 minutes on his calendar. I walked into his office; he had no idea who I was or why I was there. I gave him the 60-second elevator pitch, "I'm the best unknown junior executive in the company, and I think I can be a valuable asset to you in Sydney."

He leaned back in his chair and smiled, "Who are you again?"

During the next twenty minutes, we established primitive chemistry. Joe's phone rang. He nodded, "In a few minutes." He looked at me, "Look Matt, gotta hand it to you, you've got a pair of balls, just getting on my calendar. But you're too green, and I've got to get to a Board meeting." That was that.

Over the next two years, I worked my butt off and became one of the rising stars in Y&R's account management group. A kid from the Bronx, with no Ivy League background, becoming a vice president at 33 was like the New York Jets beating the Baltimore Colts in the 1968 Super Bowl.

I was in my office barking orders when my assistant, Janet Francis, a slightly rotund, incredibly efficient, and extremely edgy, announced, "That DeDeo guy is on the phone!" I picked up the phone and said, "Now you want me to go to Australia." He laughed and suggested I come down to talk.

An hour later, the deal was struck. I would become the Number Two at the fastest growing agency in Australia with spanking new offices that overlooked the breathtaking Sydney Harbor Bridge. Explaining what I had just agreed to, to my wife was a bit tricky; we had just bought a new house that Mary Ann loved in Purchase, New York, 25 minutes from Manhattan. But in the end, she decided she was excited about "the new adventure."

~

The Sydney transfer turned out to be the experience of a lifetime, for all of us. The clients were great; the business expanded; we traveled the country seeing Ayers Rock, Perth, Melbourne, and so much more. We also bought a terrace house and lived in the elegant historic community of Paddington-Woolhara. But, as always, it was about the people. Welcoming, fun-loving, they taught me a life lesson, "Work to live, not the reverse."

We also discovered Australians love to travel, see the world. When we left, we told our many new friends to "look us up, if you ever get to the States."

They took it literally. In the first year, we hosted a half a dozen visitors, none more memorable than my friend Chris Martin-Murphy. He was a management peer in Sydney, but that's where the similarity ended. Chris was English-Irish-Australian. His mother and father met in England and relocated to Australia when he was a child. It was hilarious listening to him blend his heritage, "Bloody good show, mate." Chris was also a terrific guitar player, who wrote music; he prided himself on playing local gigs for unlimited schooners (22-ounce glasses of beer).

~

Before Chris visited, he did his homework, "I want to get a feel of the real New York." At the top of his punch list was an odd combination of the Paul Revere Tavern on Lexington Avenue and seeing a Broadway play. Chris had read somewhere that the Paul Revere was the only Manhattan watering hole where you could drink a yard of beer, a fact entirely unknown to me. I didn't even know what a yard of beer was until somebody handed me this glass bowl with a big neck. As Chris explained, "Mate, the idea is to drink the entire quart in one lift without spilling a drop."

After I embarrassed myself a few times, it was off to an 8 PM curtain at the theater. Chris asked what we were seeing. I told him I didn't know. "New York had this new half-price TKTS ticket booth, where you can buy the best remaining seats at half face value." I emphasized, "Sitting close to the stage is what makes for the memorable Broadway experience."

I noted it was the middle of the week. Chris stared as if to say, *so what*. I explained the subtleties known to true Broadway aficionados like myself. "Tuesdays and Wednesdays are what we call low-traffic days; very few tourists. We should be a lock for either *Cat on a Hot Tin Roof* or *Gypsy* (the top shows at the time)."

~

We started to walk across town to the theater district. Chris stopped, "Wouldn't it be safer to take a cab?" He explained he had read a lot of stories about how dangerous New York was at night. I laughed. "No worries. You're with a native. I know every street in Manhattan."

We cut through Grand Central Station, a tourist site in its own right. At the top of the stairs to the street; Chris saw thousands of people hustling around, massive back-lit advertising billboards, and a line at the ticket booth that stretched across the massive floor.

"Mate," he laughed, eyes bulging, "I don't think this many people live in Sydney."

We crossed Fifth Avenue and headed up 47th Street. I continued our self-guided tour, "This is the Diamond District; they say more diamonds change hands here every day than anywhere else in the world."

The exchanges were closed, and the lights were off. Chris looked at the empty window displays. "Where are the diamonds?" I laughed, "Chris, this is New York. Nobody leaves diamonds in their windows overnight."

~

The Broadway lights were now in sight a few blocks away, but the last two side streets along the way were pitch black. At the last diamond exchange doorway, I saw a figure out of the corner of my eyes. So did Chris. The small dark figure appeared to be following us. Chris nervously picked up the pace, but to no avail. The footsteps got louder; the figure was gaining on us. I thought to myself *I don't even have my attaché case to take a swing when the bastard tries to rip us off.*

The footsteps were so close I could feel them. I whispered to Chris, "Let's split up, you go right, I'll go left." He nodded. Just as we made our move, an elderly woman with a Macy's shopping bag walked by the two of us. She nodded, "Good evening, boys. Nice night for a walk."

Chapter 10

Coffee Near Carnegie

SEPTEMBER 1975

Things were going well on the career front.

I was now one of the Young and Rubicam's youngest vice presidents, and managed the prestigious Chiquita Bananas account, and traveled across the United States making nice to the company's key distributors.

~

One day the phone rang. It was Ken Cantley, the Chiquita V.P. of Marketing. "I need you to join me sucking up to Louie "King" Duristanti in South San Francisco." Louie was a blue-collar multi-millionaire with a titanic ego and a well-earned reputation as a cutthroat negotiator who craved special-recognition status from Chiquita management.

Word was out that Louie, Chiquita's most visible and largest wholesale distributor, was being courted by a major competitor, Dole, to switch alliances — a move that could cost Chiquita tens of millions in lost revenues.

According to Cantley, my job was "to dazzle him with Louie-centric advertising concepts to make Dole go away."

~

The wired-haired, square-jawed, larger-than-life Louie had a serious gripe (to Louie). "I love the Chiquita guys, but I ain't getting treated big time. I saw some of those trade ads you did, why the hell are you featuring Steve Kontos in Birmingham? The King does ten times the business."

After lunch and a tour of his humongous produce facility, Louie, Ken and I were standing next to a parking lot full of white 18-wheel delivery trucks. "Nobody in the country got a fleet of refrigerated trucks like this. Even got an automatic nitrogen gas release system, so my Chiquita's don't overripen before they reach my retailers."

Cantley sucked up. "Louie, Boston (Chiquita corporate headquarters) agrees nobody treats customers like you do, that's why we like to feature you in our new national ad campaign."

Louie pleased, turned to me, "So, Adman, what's the thing?"

My warped mind answered without hesitation. "Oh, we've got a perfect new theme, 'The Banana Buyers Buy," and, as Ken said, the plan is not only to feature you in the ad campaign but to create a giant poster featuring you that can be attached to the side of your trucks."

Canley's eyes popped out of his head, as I continued to make it up.

"Louie, when we get done, you'll be a household name throughout Northern California."

Louie walked to the left side of one of his trucks. "I want one of those 30-foot posters right here." Then he walked to the other side of the truck, "and here."

"How many trucks in the fleet?"

"Sixty," Louie responded,

"Consider it done. Sixty 30-foot posters."

"Good, good. When will they be delivered?"

"That's a big order. Figure 120 days."

Louie growled. "Too long."

"How about ninety days."

"Good. I'll get my guys cracking on fixture hardware."

Ken and I looked at each other and shrugged. Louie noticed. "What? Every truck is going to need grommets installed. Those big vinyl babies will be heavy."

Ken saw dollar signs. "Louie, wouldn't paper be lighter and easier?"

"Never last as long," he replied. "You headquarters guys should stick to the office!"

Louie headed for his office while we are still staring at a truck. Louie turned, "Ken let's go into the office and talk to a few of my buyers. We'll probably need to increase our weekly volume by 50 percent, maybe more. Can you guarantee Louie the consistent inventory?"

~

On the way back to the airport, Cantley was deliriously happy and full of questions. "Do we have a new advertising theme?"

"We do now," I smiled.

"What about those posters? Have you guys ever done anything like that?" he asked.

"We have now."

"Matt, when was the last time you were in Las Vegas?"

"Never been. I'm a married guy with two young children."

"I have three, so what?"

Ken explained *his thank Matt* plan. "We'll fly to Vegas, spend the evening gambling at the new Caesar's Palace, compliments of Chiquita, then take our respective planes to New York and Boston the next day."

When we walked into the casino, Ken realized I had never gambled. "First time, eh?" Ken demonstrated the finer points of craps and blackjack. Within hours, Ken made about $4,000, and I lost almost every dollar in our savings account. I dreaded going home because my wife would kill me.

~

We got to the airport with a couple of hours to kill. (This was 1975; there were no elaborate security checks.)

Ken said, "Let's play some slots." I was embarrassed to tell him I was down to my last ten dollars. He walked to the cashier with my ten-spot and returned with ten silver dollars.

"This is going to be your lucky day," he said. "I can feel it."

I figured, "what the hell. Mary Ann was picking me up at the airport, so if landed broke, I wouldn't have to worry about cab fare."

I put the first five silver dollars in the machine — no winners! Suddenly, my luck changed. The sixth silver coin registered three oranges; a flood of silver dollars hit the catch tray. I was ready to cash out. Ken said, "one more, I can feel it."

I figured why not. If if I lose the dollar, I'm a couple of hundred or so ahead.

I pulled the handle. Three 7's, the machine started ringing, the word jackpot began flashing, and silver dollars spilled all over the floor. Fellow travelers applauded. Ken and I scooped the coins into my attaché case and headed to the cashier to covert the coins to currency.

In two flicks of the slot machine arm, I had restored our savings and had a few dollars left over for a nice quiet dinner with the wife. I decided I want to keep a couple of silver dollars as a reminder of my good fortune.

~

Two days later, I was back in the Manhattan rat race. Just finished lunch with another client, Tom Brown, at the Russian Tea Room, a few doors from Carnegie Hall. Tom loved the Tea Room's signature Chicken Kiev. He also loved the Las Vegas story.

Once outside, Tom jumped in his limo and asked if I'd like a ride back to Y&R. I waved him off. I was a beautiful fall day, and I thought a little exercise would help digest my food before some mid afternoon meetings.

There were 50 people waiting for the traffic light to change at the corner of 57th next to Carnegie Hall. Out of the corner of my eye, I noticed a black man standing quietly in well-worn clothing, holding a coffee cup. The self-absorbed New Yorkers simply ignored the poor guy.

Normally, I would have assumed he was a scam artist or an unemployed deadbeat who preferred to freelance begging rather than a structured job. Today was different. I realized God gave me the opportunity to make something of myself, and it was my turn to do something for somebody besides me. I reached into my pocket for my billfold; my fingers found their way to my two Vegas good-luck silver dollars. I decided I'd give him one; maybe it would change his luck.

The light changed, and the herd crossed the street. I walked up to the man, and said simply, "Hey buddy, maybe this will change your luck."

Suddenly, the hot coffee bounced out of the guy's cup and dotted my white dress shirt.

He scowled. "What the hell is your problem? You think every black man needs a handout?"

Chapter 11

"Hymie, You're Killing Me!"

MAY 1976

I just had celebrated my eight-year anniversary at Young & Rubicam by becoming one of the youngest senior-vice-president in account management. My account portfolio now included a number of the agency's most well-known brands with big media budgets — Jell-O, Chef Boyardee, and Manufacturers Hanover Bank, among others. (In those days executive short- and long-term compensation and bonuses were directly related to the amount your clients spent in media).

The Crisci group had gradually become the depository for smart, talented people who were considered corporate mavericks. In other words, senior executives who were brilliant, eccentric incorrigibles nobody else wanted to manage. One day, I asked the head of account management resources, Marie Mandry, a chain-smoking, mid-50's single woman, why that was? She laughed and said, "Ever looked in the mirror?"

~

One of the things I did for team morale was to take my senior people to lunch every three months at a place of their choosing — on my expense account, of course. I labeled it the Crisci Quarterly Client Status Meeting to justify billing Y&R. You couldn't have made up a more unlikely cast of characters.

Ken Robinson, who was the agency's only openly gay, black, heavily-bearded account person with a shrill, squeaky voice. Ken was intellectually inquisitive, a Harvard MBA, and had traveled to some of the world's most exotic places, despite being only 33 years old.

Moses Taylor Pyne was the grandson of the wealthy Railroad Robber Barons. He was worth a small fortune and lived on an estate in Short Hills, New Jersey. I remember his interview years prior. I asked him, "Why bother to work for a living?" His response, "I have to show my family, I'm good at something beyond spending money." Taylor, despite his slight build — he was about 5'-8" and weighed 150 pounds — could drink a case of 24 green-bottled Heinekens and play three hours of tennis at the same time.

The third member of my lunch group was Jerry Shereshewsky. A Russian Jew who graduated cum laude from Columbia School of Business. He wore thick black-rimmed glasses, had an annoyingly loud, non-stop voice, smoked and sold weed on the side, and was extremely knowledgeable about world events. Jerry had selected the Tea Room because he wanted to discuss Richard Nixon's historic speech on Russian television to the Russian people in 1972.

At this point, the only things I knew about Russia was that they wanted to bomb us from Cuba, and pudgy Khrushchev banging his shoe on the podium at the United Nations, showing the world Russians had big mouths and little feet!

Jerry sensed my trepidation. He explained the Russian Tea Room on 57th Street had a been a melting pot of the rich and famous since it opened in 1927. It was the epitome of a first-class

New York eatery: overpriced entrees, garish decor, condescending service, and brusque, impatience patrons. Jerry positioned the lunch as a culinary and educational experience.

~

In those days, there was no Yelp, so I arrived at the Tea Room's iconic red canopy with low expectations. After being fed a diet of continuously depressing news about the life in Cold War Russia in the *New York Times,* I assumed we were going to have some potatoes and beet soup in a drab, austere setting.

Jerry opened the red leather front door, my expectations quickly changed. The place looked and felt like a Tsar's treasure chest: the walls were covered with hand-painted wall coverings featuring Russian fairy tales, and the main serving area was dotted with red banquettes and brightly-polished samovars.

Jerry took a few minutes to explain The *Snow Maiden, The Frog Princess,* and *Morozko.* Taylor was bored. "Jerry, can we order?" Moments later, we were looking at eight-page menus in heavy red leather folders. The variety was impressive, the descriptions sounded delicious, and the prices were mind-boggling. I asked the waiter, "First time, any suggestions." He replied condescendingly in a thick Russian accent, "The Tea Room's Chicken Kiev is world-famous."

Jerry nodded agreement. I didn't even ask what Chicken Kiev was. About 15 minutes later, a breaded chicken leg appears with some boiled red cabbage on a hand-painted plate the size of a football field.

"Good, huh? asked Jerry. The others waited for my reply.

In order not to offend Jerry, I replied ambiguously, "Never tasted anything like this." Privately, I thought to myself, *thank Christ, Y&R is paying for this kingly repast.*

~

As we ate, I noticed the room was filled primarily with older, well-heeled women, dressed to the nines. The lone exception was the two guys — Hymie and Sol — sitting at the next banquette. Hymie was bald as an eagle with a handlebar mustache, nattily attired in a blue pin-striped double-breasted suit with a pocket-watch dangling from his vest. Sol was mundanely dressed in a wrinkled gray suit, a stained ring around his shirt collar, and salt and pepper hair. The facial stubble suggested Sol hadn't shaved in days. Their table was filled with a wide variety of foods on small plates. At Tea Room prices, they had to be spending a bomb, not including dessert and coffee.

Sol spoke first, "Hymie, I thought we should talk "

"Sol, must be a serious talk, you never spend on lunch," kibitzed Hymie.

"Hymie, how long have I been buying fabric from your mills?"

"Twenty-one years."

"And how many yards?"

Hymie picked up a manila folder at his side. "Says about 58 million yards, give or take."

"Would you say I'm a good customer?" asked Sol.

"What do you think?" responded Hymie, brusquely, with a shrug of the shoulders.

"So, this year Sol orders another million yards of the same blue and gray fabric. And what do I see?"

"What?" said a disinterested Hymie, opening the caviar jar to top his smoked salmon. "Again," he says, frustrated. "I tell them Royal Otressa, and they serve me that crappy Beluga." (Otressa is $160 an ounce; Beluga $90 an ounce).

"Hymie, forget the caviar. You charged me a *tenth of a cent* more per yard. That' s a $1,000."

"Sol, salaries go up, the price of gas goes up. Pass the cost on to your customers. You think somebody is going to complain about spending another five dollars on one of your $300 Gucci knockoffs?"

Sol started to negotiate. "Hymie, I've got a reputation. I can't go around raising prices. Let's split the cost increase. I'll give you $500."

An exasperated Hymie exploded. "Sol, you're killing me!" Everybody in the restaurant looked over.

Sol said, "To be continued, I've got to go to the bathroom." In Sol's absence, the bill arrived. Best I could tell was about $825 and change. Hymie took out a thousand-dollar bill and told the waiter, "keep the change."

Chapter 12

Ya Shudda Told Me!

JUNE 1977

It was about 8 AM when I walked out of Grand Central Station on the Lexington Avenue side. I was right on time for breakfast with Angelo LaMantia, division president of global marketing giant, Unilever Company, at the UN Plaza Hotel on 44th Street and First Avenue.

Angelo loved the place! As far as he was concerned, the twin-44 story glass and green marble towers — known to insiders as UNP — was a great place to observe "third-world diplomats with huge entourages and unlimited expense accounts burn through their country's limited resources."

I had just returned from a fabulous weekend in London, where my wife and soulmate, Mary Ann, and I celebrated our 13th anniversary without the kids and the dog. She shopped like crazy at

Harrod's in Knightsbridge while I picked up my long-awaited, custom-made suit tailored by the king of Savile Row, Edward Sexton.

For a kid from the Bronx, turned Madison Avenue hot-stuff, Sexton had changed my life on a prior business trip to London after one visit to his meticulous shop that reeked of royalty. Besides being a great tailor, Sexton was a sophisticated salesman. The signed pictures on his walls reinforced the obvious — Edward was the bespoke tailor of royalty for more than three decades.

Edward quickly identified my needs. A man in "my position of influence" should settle for nothing less than Sexton signature single-breasted, pointed-lapel $6,000 suit and $500 shirt with white collar and French cuffs. He sucked up so brilliantly that I decided to order two of each.

~

When I arrived at our usual corner table, Angelo noticed immediately. "Nice threads. You look very British."

The next 90 minutes saw two modestly overweight, middle-aged men flinging friendly barbs while wolfing down the UN Plaza's house specialty, lox baked into a three-egg omelet resting on a bed of arugula and topped with a hint of Black Sea caviar.

The time flew by. It was 9:30 AM, and my next (9:45) meeting at Bristol Meyers Headquarters on Park Avenue, was 14 blocks away. Normally, I would have walked and digested my food. But the BM Marketing S.V.P., Geoff Lehman, was a royal pain in the ass who was convinced that advertising agencies were necessary evils. Geoff also believed his $50 million+ marketing budget gave him the inalienable right to rag on his agency's management — me — at least once a month.

~

"No sweat," I thought to myself. There are always cabs outside the hotel. Oddly, on this particular morning, the doorman was nowhere to be found. Fortunately, there was a line of 20, maybe 25, cabs waiting to my right that stretched up the entire block to Second Avenue. From experience, I knew that line meant one thing — the cabbies had been waiting a while for a passenger.

The first cab was a big, old yellow checkered cab with legroom and air conditioning. I jumped in, computer bag first.

"Good morning," I smiled. The cab driver, a rotund man with hands big enough to twist a lead pipe, nodded and gave me the New York once over.

"I'm in a bit of a hurry. I'm running late for a meeting at 52nd and Park. I know it's a short hop, but I'll make it up to you in the tip."

The cabbie sneered as we pull away from the curb. He stared in the rear-view mirror.

"Hell of a set of threads, where'd you get them, Bud?"

I noticed his license and ID near the front dashboard read Ernest Martini.

"Just picked them up in London, Ernie."

"You in from London?"

"Yeah, just got back last night."

Without warning, Ernie turned into a fire-breathing Doctor Jekyll. "You god-damn out-of-town diplomats in your fancy suits! You have no freakin' idea how hard it is to make a buck in this freakin' city."

Ernie started complaining to the picture of a beautiful young lady scotch-taped to his dashboard. "Marguerite, I know, I know. Grandpa promised you money for college so that you could have a better life. I'm doing my best."

Ernie hadn't heard me say, "the I'll make it up in the tip." I tried to remind him, but Ernie was on a roll. He wailed at a small plastic Jesus dangling from the arm of his rear-view mirror. "Sweet Jesus, why do you always give me the big shots with $5-dollar rides." Then he mumbled something about being a faithful Catholic, a loyal member of his flock.

~

I decided to push back, diplomatically. "Ernie, I understand the problem. That's why I told you when I got in I'd make up for the short ride with a good tip." I paused. "And, for the record, I'm not from out of town. I was born in Harlem, raised in Fort Apache in the South Bronx. Dad was a butcher and Mom was a telephone operator. They saved their pennies, so I could get a good education, a good job, and afford to treat my wife to a 25th anniversary trip to London."

~

"Bullshit," says Ernie in a pique of disbelief. "I'm from da Bronx. You don't sound like me."

I pushed back. "So that's my fault?"

"Good comeback. You got balls, buddy. What's your name?"

"Mathew."

"Like one of the twelve apostles," responded a suddenly transformed Ernie. "Nothing personal, Buddy, but I can smell a real New Yorker from a mile away."

Suddenly, Ernie turned into the 20-question man.

"Where in Harlem?"

"124th Street and 11th Avenue."

"Near the El (overhead subway)?"

"No, down the block by Nick's barber shop."

"And, you lived in Fort Apache?"

"141st and St. Ann's Avenue."

"Ever go to the movies?"

"Yeah, I used to catch those cowboy double features on Saturday at the RKO Royal theater near Third Avenue and 149th Street."

We stopped for a light. Ernie turned around with a big smile on his face. "So, you really are from here?"

~

About halfway to my meeting. Ernie became a tour guide. "What do ya think of my cab? Matty, the shtick. The picture of the kid?"

I assumed he was fishing for a compliment. "Your granddaughter's cute. How old is she?"

Ernie started to laugh. "My granddaughter? I ain't married. It's for show. You know, I talk to the kids, make the passengers feel sorry. Always bumps the tips. But the international crowd from the United Nations. They're a choice piece of cake; that's why I hang out here. The money drips out of their pockets. Three trips with those guys bring more tips than a whole day in midtown."

Ernie opened the glove compartment and handed me a half a dozen pictures of kids. "I rotate my family every day. Ernie is always trying to figure out which kids have the best tip appeal, if you know what I mean."

Now Ernie had me laughing. "Market research is a great tool. Use it in advertising all the time to figure out how to sell people more things than they actually need."

Ernie smiled devilishly. "Know what I've learned? Small kids mean small tips. Big grandkids needing college money means big tips."

"What about Jesus?"

"There's this guy with an outdoor stall on 128th Street and Adam Clayton Boulevard. He sells Jesus in all sizes and colors. I just choose a conservative Jesus, I want to seem real religious. Fact is, I ain't been to Church in years. Got the idea listening to Reverend Billy Sol on Imus." (The politically incorrect and highly controversial Don Imus Show was New York's most popular morning radio show for more than a decade.)

I smiled and started to tap my foot rhythmically, "I don't care if the rain go freezin' so long as I have that plastic Jesus on the dashboard of my car." Ernie joined me in a refrain of the chorus, tapping the dashboard. I looked at my watch.

"Ernie, I almost forgot…the damn meeting!"

"No worries, Matty. The guys you're meeting, ball busters, right?"

Ernie made a sharp turn, cut between two trucks and ran a red light before coming to an abrupt halt. "Here we is, right on time," said Ernie, proudly."

The meter read $6.40. I took out a $20 bill and handed it to Ernie. "Keep the change. Like I said when I got in, I'd make it up to you."

Ernie handed the twenty back. "Your money's no good here. This trips on me. Ya shudda told me!"

Chapter 13

30-Ounce Porterhouse

MAY 1979

New York-born Bill LaPorte, a graduate of both Princeton and Harvard, was a business legend in America, and I was about to lunch with him at New York's legendary Manny Wolf's Chophouse on East 49th Street.

Under Laporte's leadership, his company, American Home Products (AHP), advertised aggressively on television and became one of the largest producers of pharmaceuticals, prepared foods and household chemicals in the world. Products such as Anacin, Preparation H, and Chef Boyardee became household names.

LaPorte stories were legend about him running the multi-billion-dollar company with an iron fist. One of the more intimidating facts was that he approved all expenditures over $1,000. So every day a stack of invoice and requests for spending were piled in plain view on the corner of his desk. Everybody knew it wasn't possible to look at every invoice, but LaPorte was known to make the occasional "spot" call to ask a manager about a spending issue. The mere threat of receiving such a query insured every AMP manager double-checked every invoice — which was LaPorte's objective.

~

One morning my boss, Chairman Ed Ney, himself a Madison Avenue legend, called to tell me he'd arranged a lunch date for me to meet LaPorte. "Bill heard you're the new guy." Ney was all about strong client-agency at the senior management levels.

Ed offered a few cautions in his raspy voice. "Remember he's a 66-year old conservative Republican, and you're one of those thirty-something liberals. And Bill's all about the business. Make sure you know every key issue on every brand before you walk in there — he loves to intimidate people."

On the cab ride over, there was the usual traffic jam heading up Third Avenue, so I arrived about five minutes late. The maître de, John, said "Your guest is in the side dining room. He requested a quiet corner table." John walked me to the table where a distinguished gentleman in a dark pin-striped blue suit, starched white shirt, and red club tie, was sitting.

"Nice to meet you, Mr. LaPorte." I smiled and stuck my hand out. He gave me the once over and glared. "I'm sorry about being late, the cab…" He interrupted, "Son, you're late. Not a good way to start." I remembered Ed's advice, get right down to business. "My staff and I were looking over the Chef Boyardee numbers yesterday, and…" He again interrupted, "Your staff? Don't *you* review *my* numbers? Hell, we spend enough with you guys to get your undivided attention."

~

La Porte picked up the menu. "Let's order. I don't like to talk business on an empty stomach." He scanned the extensive menu. "Christ! Look at these prices. Can't believe they've lasted 70 years." He picked the cheapest item on the menu, a steak burger and fries. I did the same. The waiter asked if we'd like a drink or a glass of wine. "Never drink at lunchtime," responded LaPorte.

~

Four heavyset guys walked in and sat down at a nearby table. They ordered a pitcher of double martinis. Minutes later, the waiter walked by with four steaks so large they hung off the plates. A second waiter followed with baked potatoes the size of Idaho, a bucket of creamed spinach, and a mountain of breaded onion rings.

Before long they were talking so loudly I realized they were negotiating the purchase of a hundred 18-wheel refrigerated trucks for somebody's wholesale distribution business.

LaPorte shook his head. "Now that's stupid, son, never negotiate in public on a full stomach!" He ordered coffee, passed on dessert, and pulled six sheets of paper, scotch-taped together out of his breast-pocket. He spread the sheet on the table. It was company sales-by brand-by-region-by-month for the last 18 months. There were hand-written scribbles everywhere.

LaPorte's finger came to rest in Chicago. "Did you see that sales trend for Chef Ravioli in the Chicago sales district? Down 12 percent, six months in a row. Any thoughts?" I take an educated guess. "Not sure, but Chicago is a Franco-American (main competitor) stronghold."

Never thought of that," he replied. "Tell Jaicks (AHF Food Division President), "maybe we should increase the media budget and lower the price until they go away." By the time LaPorte finished the grilling, my shirt was a mass of perspiration. Fortunately, my suit coat masked the problem.

He put the crumpled paper back in his pocket, stood up and smiled, "I've gotta get going. But it was nice to meet you." We shook hands. The heavyset guys with the drinks and food were now eating cheesecake.

"Son, you did better than most. I'll tell Ed you're a keeper." LaPorte looked at the bacchanalian feast next door. "Just remember what I said, never be late, know the numbers, and forget the martinis and 30-ounce porterhouse."

Chapter 14

Leonard M.D.

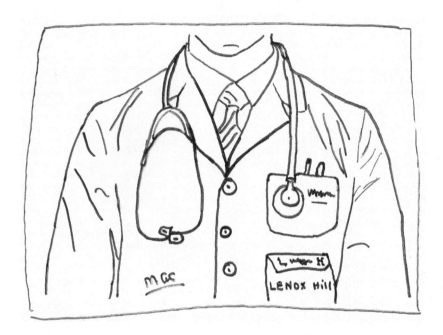

DECEMBER 1980

My relationship with Leonard began shortly after my 40th birthday, a dark moment that marked my official entrance to middle age.

Ironically, the day after my surprise party (I hate surprise parties), one of the celebrants, my friend Ben Wolfe, dropped dead of a heart attack shoveling the driveway of his weekend get-away in Rye, New York.

That night I reflected on Ben's sudden death in the living room staring silently into the crackling fire swirling a Calvados (French Apple Brandy). Mary Ann sensed something was wrong.

Ben's death was a wakeup call to take better care of myself. I hadn't had a physical in years; in fact, I didn't even have a doctor. Mary Ann suggested Leonard DeRi, an internist whom she worked closely with at Misericordia Hospital (her employer). DeRi also had offices in the East 70's near Lexington Avenue, which made sense for me, given my typically long days at work.

Mary Ann had an additional observation, "He's a lot like you" — whatever that meant.

~

The next day I made an appointment with a sultry voice that belonged to a woman who introduced herself as Louisa.

When I arrived, I was underwhelmed: the office austere — clinical white walls, a few spartan black-leather-and-chrome chairs, no pictures, and no reading materials.

"You must be Mr. Crisci," said a stunning flaxen-haired blonde with a great figure, sexy smile, sophisticated look, small cheeks, big eyes, and turned-up nose, "I'm Louisa, Doctor DeRi will be with you in a few minutes."

I mumbled under my breath cynically, *sure, the old 'he'll be with you in a few minutes' trick.*

"Sorry, Mr. Crisci, did you say something?" asked Louisa.

"No, not really."

Three minutes later, a modest-sized gentleman in a white coat appeared. "Hi, I'm Dr. D." Bald as an eagle, pudgy — about 30 pounds overweight — round face with a small button nose and a smile wide as the Mississippi. I thought to myself, is this what Mary Ann meant by "a lot like you?"

"Mr. Crisci, nice to meet you," he continued. "Mary Ann talks about you all the time. Your wife's a true professional and very much in love." He smiled warmly. "Let's go into my office and chat."

Leonard's office was an extension of the waiting room: neat, clinical white walls, and barren desk that made me wonder *does this guy have any patients?*

"You're in advertising, what do you think of my minimalist office design?" asked the doctor, enthusiastically.

I hesitated. The doctor unknowingly came to my rescue. "I told my decorator I wanted my patients to feel at home, no white-coat syndrome. This is all Johnathan — the hand-lacquered Chinese white walls, the Corbusier Comfort Chairs (super-expensive), even the antique Persian prayer rug."

I replied simply, "Agreed."

What else can you say to somebody who has just bought an expensive line of bullshit, lock, stock, and barrel?

~

We moved from offices to medicine. Dr. DeRi took an incredibly detailed profile — my daily diet, my sleeping patterns, my mental attitude, and so on; it was 45 minutes before he picked up his stethoscope. I was impressed; today, most doctors would have seen three patients in the same time.

The doctor suggested a bank of basic blood tests to get a base point. Minutes later Louisa hand-carried a half a dozen vials to the lab next store and returned with a cup of Lavazza coffee and the *New York Times.* "Why don't you just wait inside," she smiled, "The lab said they'd have the results in about 30 minutes."

About 30 minutes later, D. DeRi was pouring over Lipid panels and my HDL and LDL scores. "Bottom line, everything looks pretty good for somebody in your business."

"Does that mean I'm not going to die anytime soon?" I quipped,
sarcastically. Dr. DeRi returned the quip, "Just never know." I thought of Ben.

~

The year passed quickly. It was again time for my annual physical, and maybe a flu shot. To my surprise, Dr. DeRi remembered me as a patient, a person, and the purveyor of bad jokes.

"Doctor, I didn't mention this last year, but I do have an issue I'd like to discuss. I was in a major automobile accident at ten and have lived with chronic neck pain since, not horrible, but just enough to be uncomfortable."

Leonard nodded understandingly and examined my neck area. "Since there are no prior records, let's do an MRI, just to make sure I don't miss anything."

About two weeks later, I returned to the doctor's office to get the results. Louisa took my blood pressure. It read 203/105. "Whoa," she said.

"It only happens when I see you!" I cracked.

Louisa didn't find my comment funny. "I'll let the doctor know."

"Mr. Crisci, I've reviewed the MRI findings. You do have a moderately ruptured disc in the neck region," said DeRi.

"And, so.....," I asked.

"As so, we have two options: you can grin and bear it, or we can do spinal surgery." He paused. "Candidly, the success rate for this class of surgery is less than 60 percent and the side effects, migraines and such, could be worse than the solution."

"What would you do, if you were me?"

"Matt," said DeRi, "Do you mind if I call you Matt?" I nodded. "Frankly, if it were me, I'd just live my life. Periodic discomfort aches and pains are just part of growing old. It's more important to maintain the right mental attitude."

I sensed we were entering a new phase of our relationship.

"You know, as a doctor, I've seen some difficult things, so I thank God every day for what I've been given: a wonderful loving wife much like Mary Ann, and two wonderful sons. My oldest, Leonard Jr., has just finished high school. If it all ended tomorrow, I'd die a happy man."

~

In the next eight years, the annual physical continued, though the proportions altered significantly. My exam filled the first 30 minutes; our personal conversations the next 90. We even compared notes on how we met our wives.

"I met Mary Ann at my first college dance when she was 16. That night, I bet my best friend John $5 I would marry her. Not only did I win the bet, but John is still my best friend, the godfather of my first son, and Chairman of the Department of Anesthesiology at New York Hospital."

"Small world, you don't mean THE Dr. John Savarese?" asked Leonard.

"I think so." I responded, curiously.

"I only know him from professional seminars and meetings. He is considered one of the world's most respected medical researchers."

"He's never once said anything. He's just my friend."

After the professional digression, we returned to family. "How did you meet your wife?" I asked.

"Nothing quite so romantic. I met Barbara in medical school. Blind date from friends, sweet lady, but our relationship took time to develop."

"You weren't sure?"

"No, I was just like you with Mary Ann, but Barbara wasn't so sure! After four years of cajoling, I grew on her," he laughed. "I think the girls would enjoy each other's company immensely. We should get together for dinner."

"I'll talk to Mary Ann. We'll pick some dates that might work." We exchanged home phone numbers and put them in our wallets.

~

Another year passed, my exam indicated I remained in good health. But despite the best intentions, we had still not had that dinner.

"How are the boys"? asked Leonard. "Mary Ann tells me they are getting big."

"True, the oldest is already off to high school. Where does the time go?"

"I know what you mean, I have a son and a daughter. Both have completed their formal schooling. In fact, my son, Leonard Jr., has just finished Harvard Medical School."

"Be like Dad," I smiled.

"No, it was totally his decision. Lenny (family nickname) and I have always been close; I consider him my best friend. But as a father I went out of my way, not to push, prod or even suggest medicine as a profession. I'm both proud and sad. Proud because Lenny is following his dream; sad because a busy doctor's life means we see a lot less of him."

Leonard looked out the window, a touch of melancholy written on his face. "I was never very close to my father. We just didn't see eye to eye; he always thought I was too damn independent, a condescending rabble-rouser. He didn't even want me at his funeral. That's why my relationship is so important to me. What about you and your father?" asked Leonard.

"We weren't very close either; but for an entirely different reason. Dad was a wholesale butcher, which meant he worked mostly at night — like 11 PM to 7 AM. The weird hours, lack of exercise, and poor eating habits contributed to his extremely obesity — he was five-foot-eight and weighed almost 410 pounds. Decent man, but he was simply unable to do the things kids like to do. We were like two ships passing in the wind, me active by day, him waddling by night. Any other close family?" I asked.

"Do have a twin brother, John. We would do anything for each other. Unfortunately, he lives 3,000 miles away in Washington. But despite the distance and my doctor's schedule, we make it our business to talk every week. Enough about me," smiled Leonard. "How is your business?"

"Life has been good.," I replied. "I'm now a big deal senior executive. Probably manage 1,000 people or so. Constantly on planes, visiting clients. Speak around the world. Just amazes me, people pay to hear what I have to say!"

Leonard laughed, an engaging twinkle in his eye.

"Leonard, you know I was thinking, we've never done that damn dinner! The good news is that I've had so much time to think about it, I've come up with an idea that might make up for eight years of inexcusable procrastination."

"I'm all ears," said Leonard.

"Let's take both families away for a weekend. The Cape, maybe Nantucket, I bet they'll have a great time together, just like us. I realize the idea is a bit more complicated than dinner, but we can make it work."

"Only if we let the ladies do the organizing. Guys stink at social organization. The way we're going, we might meet in Cape Heaven, long after the DeRis and Criscis have departed planet earth!"

Several more years passed. We discussed houses, cars, retirement, kids, wives, cats, dogs, trips, politics, current events, and even our favorite newspaper, the *New York Times* — which we discovered we read in precisely the same order: front page headlines, business, sports, local metro, and finally the decided liberal-left editorial page.

There was also the constant good-natured ribbing.

"Leonard, it's hard to believe, we've known each other 20 years. You look pretty damn good for an old, bald, doctor!"

Leonard counterpunched, "and you don't look too bad for a bald, pudgy, middle-aged businessman!"

We giggled like kids.

~

Another year passed. I was in a particularly playful mood for my annual physical. We had just landed a big, new piece of business and I was about to receive a handsome six-figure bonus.

"Leonard, we've been doing it your way for years. How about if I play doctor and you're the patient. Maybe you can pick up a few tips on bedside manner."

"I'm not sure that's such a good idea," said Leonard somberly.

Turned out Leonard had a rare form of leukemia, in remission for years, which had returned with a vengeance. His only hope — a complicated bone marrow transplant with a donor match.

"Thank God for my brother John in Washington. The surgery is scheduled in four weeks; I'm getting weaker by the day."

I was speechless. Ill-defined, incomplete, uncapturable thoughts whirled inside my head.

Leonard didn't want pity. "Fine doctor you are," chuckled Leonard. "You never even noticed your patient was dying."

For some inexplicable reason, the two of us laughed uncontrollably for the next five minutes. When the laughter subsided, we held each other tightly and cried. As I left, I wished my friend Godspeed and said I would call the office every day for a status update.

~

Somehow, once again, the weeks flew by as life got in the way. I was buried in the bullshit of work and lost sight of what was important. One evening as I sat in yet another superfluous meeting, lightning struck! *My God, I never called Leonard.* I bolted from the chair, dashed to a phone and called Leonard's office. "Louisa, this is Matt Crisci, I'm calling to check on Leonard. How did the surgery go?"

A calm, detached voice responded, almost like a computer recording, "The surgery, though tedious, went well enough, both brothers exited safe and sound. Five months went by, and the worst seemed over. The Doctor made plans to return to work. Unfortunately, the leukemia returned, more savage than ever. Knowing his time was short, the family decided to keep the office because so many patients like yourself have called and written notes. The continuous outpouring is a testament to what a special doctor he was. The family would like to thank you for your interest."

I was guilt-stricken. *Five months ago, we hugged, and I promised. How stupid and selfish could I have been? How do you love someone, then never think beyond silly, meaningless day-to-day activities? What an absolute jerk!*

Then pissed. *After all Leonard and I shared, how could Louisa typecast me as just another patient? What a Goddamn insult!*

At that moment I realized the fault was mine. We never had the dinner. We never made the trip. I turned insecure; *maybe the friendship was more imagined than real?*

I thought long and hard about what was appropriate. I convinced himself that a handwritten note was best. A follow-up would depend upon the reaction I received, if any. As I began to write a warm note to an acquaintance, something happened. My pen became a self-propelled instrument fueled by unconditional love. I could hear the angels pleading, More, much more. My hand finally came to a stop, tears rolled down my cheek and landed on the letter, making the salutation, "Cordially, your friend Matt" unreadable.

I mailed the note there, embarrassed it had taken me 20 years to understand the fragility of friendship. The next morning, I left on a business trip to Peoria, Illinois, to visit some key retail accounts. On my way back to New York, I called Mary Ann to make small talk, "So, how was your day? Anything interesting happen?"

"As a matter of fact, yes," Mary replied. "Leonard called earlier today. He left his phone number".

I was excited. Our friendship was real. "Give me this number, I'll call him as soon as I get to the airport and find a quiet spot in one of the lounges." This time, I kept my word. After I checked in, I headed straight for the telephone. *God damn it,* somehow, I lost the paper with Leonard's number. I called home. *Double damn! No answer.* I called telephone information. The number was unlisted!

I post-rationalized, I'd call as soon as I got home. The plane ride would give me time to develop a proper response to Leonard's almost certain question, "where've you been, buddy?"

Four hours later, I arrived home. Fortunately, the number was still on Mary's notepad. I hugged and kissed the kids, then dashed up to my office to call Leonard.

The phone rang, five maybe six times, it seemed like an eternity. Finally, a sweet, kind woman's voice answered, my intuition told me it was Barbara.

"May I say hello to Leonard. I'm an old friend, a former patient.

"Sorry," she said in a whisper, "Leonard passed away about two hours ago."

I began to sob.

The voice said, "Is this Matt?"

"Why yes."

"This is Barbara. I was there when he made that last call to you."

The last call to you! The last call to you! The last call to you! The last call to you!

~

About six months later, I arrived home early and decided to pick up Mary Ann at the hospital. When I reached the front desk, I asked the receptionist to page Mary Ann rather than wander around the halls looking for her.

While I was standing in the lobby, I noticed a likable-looking young doctor in a white coat waiting for an elevator. He was bald as an eagle, slightly pudgy, with a smile as wide as the Mississippi. He also had a round face, small button nose and a twinkle in his eye.

I stared at the man for about a minute. Our eyes met mine. Instead of entering the elevator, the man walked over to me.

Hyper-concerned my staring offended the guy, I spoke first. "I'm sorry about the staring, but you remind me so much of a dear doctor friend who passed away."

The man just smiled and said, "I understand. You must be Matt?"

I stood speechless, frozen in space.

"I knew the doctor well. Leonard was my dad. I'm Leonard Jr. I believe Dad talked about me?"

I nodded with pride, and embarrassment.

"Dad spoke of you often as we were growing up. I know you were special friends, he told me all the things you shared with over the years. Unfortunate you and Mary Ann and my Mom and Dad never had that dinner, nor did our families ever that that trip. I don't know how many times Dad mentioned those plans."

I was speechless and humbled.

"After that last call, Dad said, 'Leonard, when you meet Matt, tell him everything's okay. Tell him, I'll take care of the family outing. We just have to change the location.'"

Chapter 15

JELL-O Bowl II

JUNE 1981

One of the things Y&R Chairman Ed Ney always stressed was that strong client-agency management relationships were the cornerstone of account longevity in an industry known for client loyalty.

As I rose through the ranks, I passed the *Gospel According to Ney* to all my direct reports. In time, I came to manage the largest single brand group in the agency, the high-spending General Foods Corporation, headquartered in White Plains, New York — acquired years later by Kraft Foods for billions. The account contained well-known household names like Maxwell House Coffee, Stovetop Stuffing Mix, and Cool Whip, among others. But none was more well-known and respected than the Jell-O brand. Not surprisingly, the client stocked the brand management group with cream-of-the-crop MBA's from the Ivy League Schools and Wharton.

~

Under my stewardship, things went well at both the management and everyday levels. The two groups worked as a team, got to know each other socially, and always had each other's back.

Summer was coming. During my bi-weekly meeting with Division manager Ed Collier, I suggested we carve out a day for a client-agency mini-Olympiad, followed by sandwiches and beer. Ed liked the idea: he thought it would be a worthwhile team-building exercise. We agreed on non-taxing sporting competitions that would allow everyone to compete. We picked a local park not far from General Foods headquarters, where people could play volleyball, bean bag toss, and a basketball matching-shot game called *Horse,* using a seven-foot high backboard, instead of the regulation 10-foot-high backboard. Ed and I selected managers for each game.

There were about 50 participants. We decided to give the event a name — The Jello-0 Bowl, parody on the NFL Super Bowl — established a scoring system and awarded some small prizes to the winners during the post-Olympiad sandwich social. To my surprise, the event, pictures, and results were publicized in client and agency company-wide newsletters. My boss, the new Y&R President Alex Kroll — a Rutgers University All-American drafted by the New York Jets — wanted to know why the agency lost to a bunch of "Ivy softies."

~

In the spring of the following year, two of my top account supervisors, Tim Timmons and Frank Vuono, themselves former college athletes, proposed some significant upgrades for Jell-O Bowl II. "We've got 100-150 people who want to sign up," said the six-foot-three-inch Vuono, towering over my desk. "I think General Foods has a like number." Vuono proposal: a round-robin preliminary round followed by sudden-death final in four different sports. He estimated the competition would take most of the day.

I thought to myself, great idea. *Wait till Kroll hears I want to take a hundred Y&R people out of the office for the day.*

But the guys were not finished. "After the games, we think there should be a catered barbecue dinner (Vuono came from a long line of Italian foodies) with live music, drinks, and cocktails."

"Bet you already have a park in mind." I smiled.

"Done," said Timmons, waving a piece of paper. . "We got a permit to close the Shippan Seaside Park in Stamford."

"Why Stamford?"

"It's close to your house," said Vuono. "We figured the grounds, the pool, the tennis court. It's perfect!" We'll have people bussed from the park to your place and organize cabs to take them home after they get sloshed."

"You guys are crazy."

Timmons continued, "And check this out. We've lined up two camera crews to film the day and evening AND my uncle, John "God" Facenda, the official voice of the NFL, has agreed to be the voice-over narrator."

The dollar signs got bigger.

"During the party, we'll award engraved trophies with the winner's names," aid Vuono. "You'll be the master of ceremonies!"

"How the hell are you going to do that?"

Timmons smiled. "The engraving shop has agreed to work overtime."

"Of course," I said cynically. "But what about the event logo and team uniforms?"

Vuono smiled. "Done, Boss, here's the logo." We think it's pretty damn good. But, I assume you were joking about uniforms. That's a little over the top."

"Thank, Christ," I commented.

"We just got Y&R and Jell-0 brand shirts with the logos and players names. Tim and I thought that should be good enough."

I didn't know whether to laugh or cry. I stood paralyzed.

"Boss, I know what you're thinking," continued Vuono. "But we pulled a lot of strings, the whole thing — including the catering for 300 people — will come in under 100k, split 50-50.

I figured if I asked Kroll for that kind of number, he'll want to have me committed. "Fellas," trying not to dampen their spirit, "Let me think about it."

~

Jell-O Bowl II, as envisioned, was a great idea. But I knew I had to get a financial partner. Two days later, I explained the concept to Collier, who surprised the hell out of me. "A 100k for all that? Let's do it. Just bill the thing as an official production job but bury the catering as a line item. Accounting never reviews line items."

Timmons and Vuono had an official Y&R production estimate created exactly as agreed. The production department, thinking they were preparing a client film estimate, automatically added the customary agency commission of 17.85 percent. When I presented the invoice to Collier, I explained I thought I could get the agency to wave the commission.

Collier would have none of it. He signed the invoice on the spot. "With all the work your guys have put into this," he said, "the commission can't possibly cover costs. How about I get accounting to expedite payment, so you can keep your out-of-pockets to a minimum."

~

Jell-O Bowl II was wildly successful. The teams battled like dogs on the fields in their personalized uniforms; there were scraped knees, bumps, cuts, and bruises. We even had a bi-partisan client agency group compile the event scoring.

The caterer worked closely with my Mary Ann, so when the buses pulled into the driveway, barbecue chicken, steaks and mountains of peeled shrimp were waiting, and the 30-foot bar by the pool was stocked to the brim, and 300 plus people danced on the tennis court to the music of the three-piece band floating in our pool. At about 3 AM, the last guests were poured into cabs.

The client feedback was incredible. Ed asked for copies of the film and hundreds of t-shirts for participants and employees. I had supplemental invoices cut and they paid the bill promptly, including the agency commission.

I didn't say much about the event in the weekly senior management meeting other than we had a successful Jell-0 II Bowl. Kroll glared across the room. "Christ, this is a business, not a social club." All eyes were on me. "Understood," I said.

A few days later my ashen-faced assistant walked into my office. Alex wants to see you right now!"

Alex was circling his table like a raging bull when I entered. "Jesus Christ," he blurted, "I just came from the General Foods annual meeting. They showed a goddamn Jell-0 Bowl II movie, calling it model of client-agency relationship building. I couldn't believe what I saw. How much did that shindig cost us?"

"The client paid for the whole thing," I replied cautiously.

He glared again.

"I'm not talking about the film. I'm talking about the WHOLE damn thing, the party, the shirts and all that other stuff.

"Like I said, they paid for the WHOLE thing. We also received full agency commission as a production job."

Kroll shook his head, "Crisci, you are some piece of work." I smiled.

"Are there any of those damn t-shirts left for me to give the Board?" glared Kroll. I nodded.

Kroll wasn't finished. "Who won?"

"We did."

That was the only time Kroll ever smiled in my presence.

Chapter 16

Time to Say Goodbye

DECEMBER 1982

The media dubbed it the 1980s the "Me" generation, and I caught the bug.

I had 15 great years at Y&R; I was now one of the ten top executives in a firm of almost 6,000. I lived in a big house with a big mortgage, big swimming pool, a tennis court I didn't play on, and five acres of land I didn't need. We traveled the world when we wanted, and I had most of the toys one could ever want or need.

The phone rang. Janet announced to the floor "It's John Vopen, — the guy you fired a few years ago for smoking dope in his office." Despite his affection for drugs, John was a creative businessman. My hope was that he had landed on his two feet.

"Matt," said John, "suppose I told you that you were one breakfast away from becoming filthy rich — not in ten or twenty years when your Y&R and deferred comp accumulated — but right now.

The idea sounded preposterous, but John knew how to push buttons. According to John, a *slightly* tarnished member of the Wall Street elite, Bob Golfman, wanted to launch and build a new public company based on an industry aggregation strategy. "He needs a squeaky-clean front man who knows what he's doing to run the operation." John chuckled. "That's you in spades!"

According to John, Golfman planned to raise the first $6 million with a concept company IPO to validate the aggregation strategy, then quickly follow with a series of additional public financings to acquire companies that fit the strategy. Initial profit growth would come from the elimination of duplicate administrative functions.

"Validate what kind of strategy?" I asked John.

John responded, "Not my place. Bob will answer that."

Initially, I resisted. "John, I'm making pretty damn good money."

John turned up the pitch. "Calling Matt. This is John. I worked at Y&R. Your comp is chump change compared to the market value of six million shares of stock, double the salary, and all the glory that comes with being known as a successful Wall Street entrepreneur."

Then he added a sweetener. "And, you approve all your own expenses."

~

I was hooked — at least for one meeting at the Sutton Place coffee shop on 54th and First. It turned out that Golfman was quite a character — impatient, egomaniacal, self-effacing, and refreshingly blunt. He talked about the hundreds of millions he'd made and lost, his planes, his estates, his bout with cocaine, his fall from grace. Most of all he talked about the need to do it one more time, "make it all back, plus some," and the business strategy.

"We're going to consolidate the excess inventory market. It's populated by a bunch of private blue-collar millionaires who, according to my research, can be aggregated into an attractive public business that throws off lots of cash."

"What makes you think they'll sell?"

"Oldest reasons in the world, greed and recognition."

He paused. I assumed it was my turn to provide some background. He interrupted, "Forget it; I've already done an extensive check. I know all about your rise at Y&R, your Mafia uncles, your Connecticut estate." He laughed. "You're the perfect fit. Straight, but not too straight." His candor was oddly refreshing.

"I think the real question for you and your family is to get comfortable with Bob Golfman. Go check me out, take your time. There's tons of stuff about me, good and bad."

I responded, "John said there was a certain urgency."

Bob responded in Bobspeak. "Forget about John. Take your time. You've got two weeks to decide. Guys like me don't come along every day."

~

After a bit of soul-searching, I decided to take the plunge. I figured worst case, if the venture blew up during the next three years, I would still be only 44 years old, and I could find my way back to a big paying job on Madison Avenue.

"Honey," I rationalized to Mary Ann, "Having big-time public operating experience will only make me more valuable to one of several major agency networks."

Two weeks later, we were sitting in Bob's elegant Sutton Place penthouse. My research indicated everything Bob said about Bob was accurate, right down to him being the subject of a front-page story in *New York Magazine*. The guy was considered a brilliant stock-market charlatan who knew how to turn ideas into prodigious sums. He also knew how to live life to the fullest and burn through prodigious sums. I gave him a rundown of my findings. "Guilty, as charged," he smiled.

We spent the next few hours eating bagels and lox with caviar while we developed the terms of a stock equity deal and employment contract with all kinds of incentive clauses.

There was only one last thing to do.

~

Y&R's gracious chairman, Ed Ney, had been like a father to me for 15 years, so telling him I was about to leave was no party.

I walked into his office as he was hanging up the phone. He leaned over and pressed the little button on the side of his desk. Eerily, the door closed. "Since you called the meeting, I thought we might want a little privacy."

I nodded. Gracious as always, Ed smiled, "I haven't had time for breakfast yet. Can I offer you something."

I shook my head nervously. "You're not going to put the touch on me for another raise, are you?"

I shook my head. "An opportunity has come my way that can change my life forever." Ed raised his eyebrows. "I have the chance to be the co-founder of a public start-up with a man who has been around the block a number of times."

"So, it's not another advertising agency?"

"No, I'm entering the world of Wall Street mergers and acquisitions. The company will be focused on turning the remarketing of excess inventory into a mainstream enterprise."

"I don't know anything about that business, but I know Wall Street can be a rough place."

"So is advertising."

"It's different. They don't play by the rules. I saw it firsthand; my brother James was an investment banker before he crashed and burned at forty-one." Ney got up. "You realize you're giving up a guaranteed future for the possibility of untold wealth."

"With all due respect, Ed, the IPO is already fully subscribed, based on my partner's reputation."

"It sounds like your mind is made up. May I offer you a little advice?"

I never forgot what Ed said next.

"There's no crime in wanting to be rich. I'd be a hypocrite if I said otherwise. But never forget, *how* you accumulate wealth can be as important as the wealth itself. I'm confident you'll achieve all your dreams, you're that kind of person. Assume your journey will be filled with forks in the road; take the wrong one, and it may be difficult to find your way back."

At that moment, I had no idea what he was talking about.

"By the way," said Ed, "Forgot to ask, what's the name of your new company?"

"Integrated Barter International, Inc.," I replied.

Ed leaned back in his chair and smiled, "Sounds like one of those made-for-Wall-Street names."

~

I never expected a bon voyage party. So when Ed told me the gang has planned a little goodbye, I took it to mean just that. To my surprise, when I walked into Barolo's in SOHO, there were 200+ agency folks and client guests. The evening felt like a roast at the Friars Club: every *Crisci-ism* created over the past 15 years was duly-noted and parodied.

As the evening ended, a red-headed creative director by the name of Janet Monte presented one final gift. "It's no secret around the agency that Matt and I have had more shouting sessions than most marriages have in a lifetime."

Every Y&R person in the room laughed.

"But in the process," continued Monte, "I've gone from his worst nightmare to his biggest supporter in the creative department. Part of Matt's magic was that he could make anybody that worked with him feel like they were the most important person in the world."

Janet handed me a hilarious caricature she created. I was sitting on a wall pulling strings attached to the agency on one side of the wall and clients on the other side." The headline read, "I feel strongly both ways."

That's an illustrated version of that poster is at the beginning of this story.

Chapter 17

Greedy, as Charged

JUNE 1983

Launching the Integrated Barter International IPO with my Wall Street mentor, Bob Golfman, turned out to be exhilarating, perplexing, unpredictable and hilarious, sometimes all at once.

Bob's advisory board, and now mine, was a bunch of characters who had lived in the world of gray so long, they were devoid of any moral compass. To them, Wall Street was about two things — money, and more money.

~

Alan Canter was the attorney. A brilliant, idiosyncratic legal mind who had consciously chosen to leave the conventional side of Wall Street for the "less monitored" Penny Stock Market. He and Bob had done a number of past deals. In many ways, Alan was

Bob's alter ego. Bob was flamboyant; Alan was calm, cool, and collected. Bob was boisterous; Alan quiet as a church mouse. Bob was a natty dresser; Alan preferred checkered wool vest sweaters over $10 white shirts he bought at the bargain-basement Alexander's Department store on 59th Street. Bob was a gourmand; the wafer-thin Alan preferred chunky peanut butter on Nabisco Saltine Crackers.

~

Marty Diamond was a Jewish kid from Queens who had somehow acquired a condescending English accent. Every sentence started with, "My boy." Bob said Marty was a brilliant financial mind and his personal strategic sounding board. Turned out, Bob was right, sort of. Marty knew all the dark side money players and all the shortcuts. He had a sixth sense about what kind of offerings excited and bored Wall Street. Whenever Bob and Marty met in person, it was behind closed doors. As I was to learn, Marty was unable to appear in our initial prospectus as a major equity holder (which he was) because of unspecified trading violations that caused him to lose all his investment licenses. And that was all Bob would ever say about that.

~

Ray and Robin Brinkman were the Wall Street version of Bonnie and Clyde. Ray was a brilliant market analyst who published corporate profiles. His job was to find the right deals, then make them "market ready" through a series of research newsletters. Despite the fact that Ray made up facts and suggested improbable revenues and profit projections, everybody on the dark side of The Street were subscribers to the Brinkman Report. They knew if Ray put his imprimatur on a startup IPO, it meant a guaranteed quick ride up, and a profitable, early cash-out.

~

Wife Robin was the perfect wife and soulmate. She was Mrs. Outside, an intimidating market-maker. She could promote anything and had a book of willing investors who had made oodles with her on prior deals. She was as pushy as Ray was reserved. As relentless as Ray was passive. When she showed up at the office — which was anytime she damn well pleased — the questions were always the same. "Bob, why can't we go faster? Bob, what's the next acquisition? Bob, give me something to feed the fish?"

~

Finally, there was Jack Fidderman. He was called a finder. On the dark side that meant he looked for deals designed for the Penny Stock Market market-makers, a collection of boiler-room salesmen who promised investors they had identified the next IBM. But Jack was much more than just a finder; he was a connector. He knew every boiler room in metro New York, and what kinds of deals the managements wanted to support. It turned out Jack identified a place for the IBI IPO: Southeast Securities across the river in Jersey City, headed by a guy who went by one name — Manuto. Manuto rode in limousines with dark tinted windows, smoked Cuban cigars, and owned a thriving boiler room with more than a hundred brokers, The room was managed by a Jewish guy named Seth, who also had no second name.

~

This unlikely cast of characters did their job. Thanks to Alan's professional diligence, the $6 million concept IPO (no financials, just possibilities) was approved by the SEC in weeks and was sold out before the end of the first day of trading. The stock jumped from ten cents to ninety cents in the first week. The following week Marty sold his 4 million shares and disappeared. The rumor was he went to Florida, although Bob would never confirm this. Two weeks later the stock price broke $2, thanks to Ray's reports and Robin's bullhorn. Jack and Manuto were happy campers.

~

As for me and my 30 million shares of stock, I was delirious, even though my holdings were 144 legend stock (founder stock that couldn't be sold until the company was public at least two years).

Sitting quietly in the spa after dinner, Mary Ann saw me staring silently at the bubbles. "You're awfully quiet," she said. "Is everything okay? Should I be worried?"

That was my moment to gloat at all the Young and Rubicam naysayers. "It's better than okay. Based on today's closing numbers, we're worth about $60 million."

She looked at me incredulously, "How can that be? The Company hasn't done anything yet."

Chapter 18

"Hey Everybody, I Know Him!"

MARCH 1984

Bob knew that the upcoming Wall Street road shows and presentations would be a rigorous grind. So being in good physical shape was mandatory.

While only a few pounds overweight, we both knew I was out of shape. Y&R client dinners and social activities had taken their toll. I probably walked once a week, maybe less. One day as we walked up the steep staircase to Ray's office, Bob noticed me huffing and puffing. "Time to fix that," he said. "It's the Vertical Club, and, I'm buying!"

~

The Vertical Club on 61st Street off First was the coolest and most expensive health club in the city at the time: seven floors of state-of-the-art health toys: machines, pools, spas, running tracks, and a fresh fruit and vegetable bar with an area to socialize. The place was also a recognized pick-up joint for the rich, successful, and beautiful people. On my first visit, Bob introduced me to a half a dozen of his regular dates. He also introduced me to Remy, a muscular trainer who Bob had organized to "jump start" my regimen.

Like all good professionals, Remy insisted we establish "a base point" to measure my progress. Bob volunteered to do 10 laps on the quarter-mile track. Remy agreed. Bob and I ran neck and neck for the first 50 yards. My legs became heavy and I started to pant. Bob finished about seven laps ahead of me. He and Remy laughed as they waited for me to finish my ten. Even Bob's honeys were laughing their asses off.

~

The public humiliation motivated me. During the next four months, I completed a morning or lunch session (depending on our schedule) every day. Remy noticed the progress. Bob didn't, until the challenge. Bob joked, "I've been paying this guy for four months, let's see what you've got. Ten laps."

This time, we ran neck and neck at a substantial clip heading into the sixth lap. I saw Bob strain as he tried to pick up the pace. I just turned on my new-found jets and blew around the last three laps. Remy and I did high-fives as we waited for Bob to finish.

~

With my physical conditioning under control, Bob focused on my wardrobe. As he explained, "On Wall Street, you've got to look prosperous; nobody invests in deadbeats. We've got some major surgery on those suits you wear from the Salvation Army thrift store."

Bob made an appointment with his famous Saville Row tailor, Edward Sexton, who was in town showing his latest styles. Sexton gave me a frightening stare at Bob's apartment. Bob noticed. "Edward, let's keep it simple, measure him just for two suits and a cashmere topcoat with the single-breasted pointed lapels you created for me."

Edward started showing me swatches. Bob interrupted. "Edward, the 120 wools, one blue pinstripe, the other gray." (120 was the thread count of the finest quality English wool).

Two hours later, we had completed all the measurements. Edward explained the bespoke process, then handed me a bill for $15,500. My eyes bulged. Bob laughed, "Crap, I've made you rich. You can afford it." He paused. "Edward, this guy also needs some new shirts." Thirty minutes later, we had added a half-dozen brightly-colored Egyptian cotton shirts with white colors and white dress cuffs. The bill was now $17,900.

~

The American Express bill came before the suits. Mary Ann had two words, "Holy shit." Fortunately for me, she decided to find out why so expensive. She discovered Edward Sexton was a bit more than Bob's tailor; he was the most revered bespoke designer in England, and virtually every male member of the Royal Family was a client.

Four months later, the clothes arrived. They fit like a glove. Bob and I had a meeting later that day with some prospective investors to determine the market appetite for a secondary $50 million offering so soon after the first. I decided to wear one of my Sexton suits and shirts and get a little exercise by walking to the meeting.

As I passed the newly completed 777 Third Avenue 40-story office building, I spotted a glassy-eyed bum with a bottle in brown bag, sitting on the ground by a white marble planter. Our eyes met; he did a double take. He got up and staggered towards me. I tried to distance myself from him.

I stood patiently at the corner traffic light huddled in the middle of waiting crowd. The bum pointed at me and yelled, "Hey everybody, I know him." The light changed. I tried to distance myself by picking up the pace. He continued to stagger behind me shouting to hundreds of curious eyes. Finally, the bum offered his insight, "Hey everybody, I know him. It's Don Rickles!"

So much for the Vertical Club and Edward Sexton.

Chapter 19

Piccarella's Chinatown

JUNE 1985

I was having a glass of wine, admiring my tennis court, kidney-shaped swimming pool, and five manicured acres. I thought to myself, *not bad for a 42-year-old kid from the South Bronx.*

My two older sons, Matt, 15, and Mark, 13, approached. Mark prodded Matt, "Ask him."

"Dad, we were thinking, this patio would be a cool place to set off fireworks on July Fourth," said Matt.

"Forget it," I replied coolly. "They're illegal in New York and Connecticut. Besides, your mother would kill me."

Mary Ann, who overheard *the men* talking blared, "You're absolutely right. Over my dead body!"

"Mom," said super-salesmen Mark, his brown curly hair blowing in the breeze, "How many times has Dad told that Louie Picarella story?'

"You know your father; it's just one of his stories," she replied.

"But suppose it isn't," posed Mark, "shouldn't we call his bluff."

Against all her better instincts, Mary Ann acquiesced. She glared, "Go ahead, make a fool of yourself. Maybe then you'll stop the stories."

~

Growing up I had two groups of friends: the well-mannered boys at All Hallows High School and the rough-and-ready neighborhood kids from the South Bronx. There was only one exception: my classmate Louie Picarella. His father was an Italian immigrant, hence the last name. His mother was Chinese with strong genes, hence he looked very Asian.

One day I sulked on a bench at McCombsdam Park across the street from the old Yankee Stadium — Louie and I threw the javelin and tossed the shotput for the track team. Louie noticed me sulking, "What the hell's your problem?"

"Money. I need to earn more than I make at the Stadium to go on the class trip to D.C. in September."

"What's the big deal? Just ask your parents."

"I don't want to get into it," I replied. "Things are really tight at home. I couldn't ask." Louie persisted. I told him about my reality.

Louie, shocked at my news, had a thought. "Maybe I can help."

My ears perked up, "How?"

"We can go into business together." I wondered what the hell he was talking about. "The timing is perfect. Fourth of July is right around the corner." I stared; he explained. "You know I just got a car."

"So?"

"So, my mom is always talking about how much she loved firework displays growing up in Chinatown. She said you could buy bottle rockets, roman candles, cherry bombs, and firecrackers on every street corner."

"So?"

"So I'm thinking to myself maybe my friend and I should drive down to Chinatown and buy some fireworks and resell them to the kids taking summer make-up courses at school. They may be stupid, but they've all got money."

"You're crazy," I said. "That's illegal."

Louie replied, "So what are the police going to do if they get catch us? Arrest us and stick us on Rikers Island with the murderers and bank robbers."

Louis had a point. So, we pooled our cash and drove down to Chinatown on a Saturday morning. The streets were a madhouse of activity. We couldn't find a space and didn't have enough extra money for a parking lot. Louis noticed a fire hydrant. "Pull into the space, and wait in the car," he said.

"Suppose the police chase me?"

"Then keep riding around the block till I get back here."

Louie jumped out of the chair and walked over two guys in their early twenties. Louie started talking in Chinese. The guy nodded his head, took the money from Louie, and they all disappeared down an alley between two buildings. Minutes later, Louie returned with two brown shopping filled with newspapers.

"You used all our money to buy newspapers!" I yelled. "Open the damn trunk!" he yelled back.

Once in the car, we started to head up the FDR. "Are you that stupid?" laughed Louie. "The bags are full of fireworks. The guy said because we were the youngest customers he ever had, we earned some extra cherry bombs." Louie put his hand in his pocket and pulled out a bunch of little red cherries with fuses. "See!" he crowed.

As we headed north, Louie explained our marketing and promotion plan. "I'll spread the word at school that you'll be sitting on the park bench, selling."

"What park bench?"

"The one from across the Grand Concourse Hotel." (16-story landmark Bronx hotel on 161st Street, not far from Yankee Stadium, where visiting players used to stay.) "That way it will be easy for them to spot you. You tell them what we've got and the prices. After they make their purchase, they can hop on the bus that stops right on the corner."

~

Louie's plan worked like a charm. The first two bags were sold out in a few days. Since we still had a week until July 4th, Louie and I decided to make a second trip to Chinatown.

I had sold about half the second stash out of my All Hallows gym bags when a policeman named Michael Hennessey approached. "Son, what've you got in those bags?"

"School books."

"Really, where do you go to school?"

"I'm taking summer classes at All Hallows on 164th Street."

"Fine Irish Christian Brothers School. I wouldn't hang around here if I were you. Somebody said there are kids trying to peddle illegal fireworks." He paused with a twinkle in his eye, "Sure'n you don't want to get mixed up in that?"

I took my bag and left. Picarella-Crisci Enterprises was history.

~

Almost 26 years later, I was getting ready to drive to Picarella's Chinatown with Matt and Mark.

Mary Ann had had one final comment as we pulled out of the driveway, "Don't call me if you get arrested!"

An hour later Canal Street was the usual chaos: streets mobbed with shoppers, honking trucks, and open-air stalls piled with fresh fish on ice.

"I think we should just park in a lot I know on Delancey Street "(about five blocks away).

"Pops," said Mark, "Let's not waste our profits. Soon, Mark spotted a space, "Over there! The other side. I'll stand in the space until you come around the block."

Minutes later, three white people — us — walked down the street carrying two empty shopping bags marked Macy's. Two Chinese guys approached from an alley between two buildings. "You shop," one said with a smile, "we sell."

"What have you got?" I asked. Everything. Rockets, Candles, Cherries. Best merchandise from China. Give you good price. Follow me." He pointed to a narrow, dimly-lit alley with a line of tin garbage pails in the distance. He started walking. We followed. The man removed the pail covers one at a time and explained the contents. "If need, more around the corner." These guys had enough fireworks to light up the Brooklyn Bridge.

The kids went ballistic. They grabbed all kinds of different stuff until their shopping bags were brimming. Money changed hands. The price was beyond fair. We started to walk back. The man stopped us. "Wait, cannot go out on street like that." He took some old Chinese newspapers and covered the top of each bag.

"Already read paper. Extra free gift, so you remember Chinatown."

Chapter 20

Hubcaps
at Fort Apache

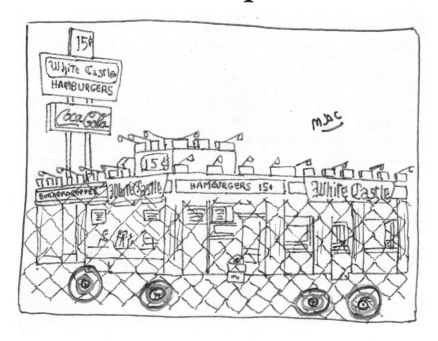

AUGUST 1987

One of the things I learned growing up in a low-income, ethnically-mixed New York neighborhood is that there are rules of survival. Anybody that tells you differently, either never lived there or is an ivory-tower demagogue. In the South Bronx, everybody knew "you gotta do what you gotta do." So that was the way I lived my formative years; never purposely seeking to hurt others but making sure I always took care of number one.

My parents struggled financially during my high school years, but they always managed school tuition, money for books, lunch, and transportation. It was unstated that finding spending money was up to me. That's why I worked at Yankee Stadium, but my earnings followed the team schedules; and that's why Louie Picarella and I sold illegal fireworks to our high school classmates, until the police shut us down.

At that point, I figured it might be better to just get a real part-time job. First up was Vinny's Market on Bruckner Boulevard, a few blocks from our apartment on 149th Street. Vinny Manucci was decent guy with a pot belly and arms thick as drainpipes, but he paid coolie wages: 75 cents an hour to wait on customers, stock the shelves, and clean the floors. So, I had no choice but to find a *more rewarding revenue stream.*

~

One night, my friend Stevie Klinger and I were slurping down chocolate egg creams at Carlino's candy store. Stevie, whose favorite movie was *The Graduate*, starring Dustin Hoffman and Anne Bancroft, smiled, then made a singular suggestion: "Hubcaps."

In those days, cars had branded hubcaps that covered the wheel- well nuts and bolts. Depending upon the car brand, the model, and condition, different hubcaps had different street values. "I know a guy that makes an extra fifty a week below the radar, if you know what I mean," said Stevie. A few days later, Stevie introduced me to Frankie Delano over vanilla egg creams. (I liked them better than chocolate.)

"I can teach youse the tricks under two conditions," said Frankie. "I get a piece of the action, and you sell the goods to my main man, Tony De Osso on Willis Avenue."

That meant Frankie double-dipped; he got something from me and something from Tony. I decided it was none of my business: "you gotta do what you gotta do." We shook hands.

~

Within two weeks I had the process down pat. Frankie would tell me what hubcaps were hot at the moment — I assume he got that information from Tony, but he never said. Stevie and I would pick a mutually convenient night and drive up to the North Bronx — where middle-class Wops, Jews, and Mics proudly parked their used cars. (There was no such thing as "previously owned in those days).

Stevie and I would cruise the less-traveled side streets, looking for the right hubcaps. The cars also had to be parked in the right place — away from the glare of the streetlights. We'd pull up to the targeted car and I'd jump out with a long screwdriver and hammer. One-two-three I'd pop the cap in the front, then the rear — you got better prices for pairs.

Like in any business, there were good and bad nights; but in the end, there were more good nights than bad.

~

To save gas money, we'd accumulated at least six pair of hubcaps at a time before we drove down to Tony's place on 137th and Willis Avenue — a small auto parts store that sat next to a White Castle hamburger drive-in. The two businesses were separated by a tall chain- link fence covered in hubcaps. The fence was Tony's for-sale catalogue. Tony was ideally located near the Willis Avenue Bridge that dumped into Manhattan, so he had a lot of impulse buyers..

I noticed little Tony was a neatnic; his store was neat as a pin, and the hubcaps were all shiny and clean. I told Stevie, "let's clean and polish the hubcaps before we show them to Tony. I think we can get a lot more for a little extra work."

One day we parked in front of Tony's around dusk. He inspected the merchandise and made an offer. I pick up the Cadillac hubcaps, "Tony, we've been doing business a long time, these are in A-1 condition. All you've got to do is hang them on the fence." He upped the offer. "Suppose we'll hang every piece, every time. You won't even need to get your hands dirty." He upped the offer again. We agreed.

Once I graduated from high school, we moved to the North Bronx, and I went off to college and got a legitimate part-time job at a bookstore. I never saw Tony again.

~

Twenty-two years later, I decided to take my sons, Matt then 12, and Mark, 10, on a tour of where "Dad grew up." But like so many memories, things are not what they once were. My parish Church, St. Rock's on 151st Street now had a big lock on the gate; my apartment house at 149th Street and Wales Avenue was now a crack den; and the basketball courts in St. Mary's Park were surrounded by chain-link fence topped with barbed wire.

The kids said very little, and Mary Ann reminded me sweetly, "Let's not forget we told the boys we'd take a ride on the Staten Island Ferry and visit the Statue of Liberty."

~

To avoid the Triborough Bridge toll, we took the Willis Avenue Bridge into Manhattan. I recalled my Tony experiences as we crawled down Willis Avenue in bumper-to-bumper traffic. Nobody believed a word. I noticed the White Castle was now a McDonald's but a rusted chain link fence still divided McDonald's and the shops next store — now all antique dealers.

I pulled over to the curb in front of the store that Tony used to own. Mary Ann protested, "Babe, I think we've had enough for the day." I paid no mind. I walked over to the chain-link fence and looked up, smiling. The memories flooded my mind.

A finger tapped me on the shoulder, "Can I help you?" asked a little gray-haired man.

"Not really," I replied. "I was just thinking about when I was a kid; I used to sell hubcaps to the guy who owned your antique shop. We'd hang them from this fence."

He stared at me. "Matty?"

"Tony!"

He nodded. I introduced Tony to the family. That was the last time anybody told me to stop with the "Dad stories."

~

It turned out Tony had never moved. The proximity to Manhattan had made lower Willis Avenue a perfect home base for antique wholesalers. "I was going to sell the store," Tony explained, "until I discovered there was a lot more money in selling old couches to rich people than selling oil filters to the do-it-yourself mechanic."

Chapter 21

"Bruce, Get in the Car"

JANUARY 1989

I had just finished a business dinner at one of New York's best (and most expensive) steakhouses, Spark's on East 45th near Third Avenue.

It was a favorite of some of my American Home Products Company senior managers; partly because of the aged New York strip steak on the bone, and partly because it was right around the corner from their corporate headquarters at 545 Third Avenue.

Spark's was also a favorite of deceased mob boss Paul Castellano, and his underboss Tommy Bilotti, who were whacked right outside the restaurant a few weeks earlier. According to reports, the two men had just finished surf and turf dinners and were waiting for their driver under the restaurant awning. Four men in beige trench coats walked up to them and opened fire.

Supposedly Gotti watched their execution in a black Lincoln sedan with tinted windows parked across the street.

The gangland murder had created a nonstop media frenzy because Gotti, nicknamed *Teflon Don*, had already been acquitted of three prior murder charges in the 80's. The question on the media's mind, could Gotti's longtime Consigliere Bruce Cutler, do it again? The acquittals, and the current intrigue was turning Cutler into a cult celebrity. His cherubic face, topped with his signature gray felt hat, appeared almost daily on front pages of the *Daily News* and *New York Post*.

I knew from my past conversations, my white-bread client, Ted Host, born and raised in Iowa, was fascinated by New York's underworld characters. As he liked to say, "you can't make this stuff up." So, it wasn't surprising that Ted chose to spend ten minutes on business, then two hours on how much I looked like Bruce Cutler. "You guys look like twins, especially since you both have round bowling ball heads and wear the same damn gray felt fedoras!"

I was not exactly pleased with the comparison, but it wasn't the first time I'd heard it. A few days before I was sitting on a New Haven North train heading to Connecticut when the guy sitting to my right leaned over and whispered, "off the record, what it's like working for John?"

I glared. He never said another word.

~

Dinner with Ted Host ended about 10 PM. I had arranged for my driver, Francis, to meet me at the corner of 46th and Second, so we could head straight uptown. I was standing at the designated spot, but Francis was a no-show. A black Lincoln sedan with tinted windows slowly pulled up next to me. The window slid down a few inches, and a firm, gravelly voice said, "Bruce, get in the car!"

I quickly responded, "I'm not who you think I am."

The voice said "Very funny, Bruce! We got a message for John."

I was scared shitless. I tried the honest approach one more time. It didn't work. The voice again spoke — this time with a little more gusto, "Bruce, get in the fuckin car! If we wanted to whack you, don't you think we would have already done it?"

Lady Luck shined down on me. Two patrolmen were changing shifts a few yards away. Calmly, I walked over to them. The gravelly voice said, "Catch you another time, Bruce," as the Lincoln burnt rubber pulling away.

I explained what just happened to officer McMahon, who had just taken over the shift. "Why don't you wait in the vestibule until your driver shows up. I'll keep an eye out just in case your friends decide to return." I did as suggested, then called Francis on my shoebox size mobile. There was no answer. A few minutes later a black Lincoln sedan with tinted windows pulled up in front of Sparks. Officer McMahon spotted the car from the corner. He pulled his gun and headed down the street. He tapped on the side of the car. The window slid down. Best I could tell he was talking to somebody.

Minutes later, McMahon waved me over. There sat Francis shaking behind the wheel, "Boss, what the hell is going on?"

"Who's car is this?" I asked.

"The Caddy had some mechanical problems, Potemkin (the lease company) was nice enough to give me a stretch Lincoln loaner with all the bells and whistles."

"Why the hell didn't you call me?"

"I got stuck in a traffic jam created by a Con Ed crew working the night shift on 24th Street," replied Francis. "My mobile was out of juice, and I couldn't just stop and call from pay phone."

McMahon smiled.

"Jesus Christ, Boss! I'm only about ten minutes late, which is pretty damn good given what I've been through."

~

As we sped up an empty Second Avenue toward Stamford, I heard my stomach growling. Francis, "pull over at the next deli, I need a cup of coffee and a bagel."

He asked, "Didn't you just eat?"

I replied, "There was some excitement after dinner, I burned all the carbs."

Tony pulled up to Wong's Korean deli on the corner of 73rd and Second. "What do you want, Boss? asked Francis."

"I'll get it," I replied. "Need to stretch my legs." Based on the earlier events, I decided to go incognito. I donned my trench coat, raised the collar, and put the gray fedora on my head. I got my bagel and coffee without incident, although two late-night patrons in the store — a woman with purple hair, and her buddy, an obvious transvestite — watched me like hawks.

"It's him," one said.

"Please, really," responded the other, waving his/her arm like a baton.

I headed to the car. They followed. As I closed the tinted glass window tight, the baton twirler said, "My God, Martha, you were right. It <u>was</u> Woody Allen."

Chapter 22

The 6:27 Express

FEBRUARY 1992

The starting routine for the 6:27 AM express train from Stamford, Connecticut, to Grand Central Station never varied: I'd grab an inky *New York Times* or *Wall Street Journal,* buy a cup of acidic, dark-roast coffee to clear the cobwebs, and head down the stairs to watch impatient fellow passengers try to keep warm by pacing up and down the open platform.

Unexpectedly, there was a strong gust of wind at my back. My *New York Times* took off down the track. "Aww, fuck." I was about to head back upstairs, when the 6:27 appeared on the horizon. I figured, this one was on time; somebody can lend me a part of their paper on the train

The train screeched to a halt. A few found the grinding of metal-on-metal disconcerting, but the majority, apparently inoculated by the routine, remained stoic and oblivious. Everybody took a final stretch at the yellow pedestrian starting line. It reminded me of the moment before the gun at a 100-yard Olympic sprint.

The train door bolted open; the starting gun sounded, the race for the gold, silver and bronze seats was underway. Gold were isle seats closest to the exit doors; Silver, isle seats in middle of the train; comfortable, not ideal. Bronze, the dreaded spot in the middle, where passengers to the right and left poked your rib cage during the entire one-hour-and-five-minute journey. Those not fortunate enough to win a medal were relegated to standing in the isle.

Today, I was lucky. I won a gold! As the train rumbled out of the platform, I watched fellow residents of the Metro North's aseptically-sealed, stainless-steel chamber, raised their newspapers to eye level and started turning the pages. The guy next to me had a *New York Times,* a *Wall Street Journal,* and a *Daily News.* "Might I borrow a section," I asked. The guy glared, "What, too cheap to spend fifty cents on a paper? Bet you drive a damn Mercedes."

~

I decided to kill some time by walking to the bathroom at the rear of the car. I noticed behind all those newspapers was nothing but blank expressions! *I think, hard to believe these are the captains of New York business and industry.* I decided to offer a cheery "good morning," to the one person who looked up. The train hit a bumpy section of track; I staggered from side to side.

"Watch my paper," he said.

~

Soon, I spotted signs of life in the last row next to the bathroom. A well-groomed woman in her early thirties was applying makeup, mirror in hand, bright red lipstick being carefully applied to a pair of sensuous lips. The train bounced again, the lipstick slid across her face and up her right cheek. She let out a painful moan and wistful sigh, then took out a tissue, cleaned the miscue, and repeated the process. She looked in her mirror. "Looks great," I said with a smile." She rolled her eyes then turned her back and stared out the window

Further down the aisle a man sat with a bagel smothered in cream cheese and jelly. My assumption: he preferred a relaxed continental breakfast on the way to Urbanland than a chaotic meal at home with the kids getting ready for school.

Another guy was drinking coffee out of sippy cup made with recycled materials and labeled "Daddy." The train hit another bump. Daddy's cup toppled over; liquid started flowing down the center aisle. To my surprise there was no coffee in the cup. It was a blend of colorful orange juice with hints of Kiwi, maybe purple grape. A pissed off passenger yelled, "get that sugar crap out of here!"

~

On my way back to my seat, I spotted a drop-dead gorgeous blonde with dark eyebrows, a chin sculpted like Michangelo's David, and dressed in a surprisingly revealing black blouse. She was wedged between two creepy-looking guys. One guy sneaked a peek, and asked, "So, what do you do?"

She gave the guy the once over, "I broker (sell) art at a gallery at fifty-seventh."

He figured he was making progress, "Much money in that?"

She feigned offense. "Do you always ride trains asking woman, how much money they make?"

The guy became flustered.

"Relax," she smiled. "I was just having fun with you. Guys today are so insecure." She continued, self-confidently, "February-March is my slow period. Most of my big hitters head to the Caribbean for sun and sand. But, when they return, I know they're good for least another seven-figure purchase."

The guy started to pull a business card out of his wallet. She kept flirting, "I'm pretty fortunate, my commissions allow me to go where I want to, when I want to go. I prefer to make my own rules."

I could tell the guy was aroused. He handed her his card. "I'm Bill, maybe we can have lunch one day?"

"I'm Sylvie," she smiled. "I don't think so. My husband would kill YOU."

~

Al, the 6:27's smiling conductor for the last eight years, entered the car. "Good morning and good day."

I nodded and returned the smile, then looked around. Heads remained buried in their newspapers. Al continued, like the greeting has been returned. "Thanks for choosing the Metro North. Here's today's weather report. Some clouds in the morning, chance of rain, maybe pick up an umbrella when you exit the train. Sunny by lunchtime, so enjoy your meal. Crisp and clear this evening, perfect weather for the ride home, and an after dinner walk with the family."

Finally, Al's warm and caring manner caused a break in the silence. A few passengers looked up and nodded. And one — the guy with the bagel — actually smiled and said "thanks."

As soon as Al left, the blank expressions returned. You could sense the thought on everybody's mind, *not long until we enter the ultimate coliseum, the "Stadium of Manhattan."*

Soon, we crossed the last body of water at 138th Street, a filthy puddle called the East River. I did a final passenger check for a bit of refreshment. Two seats in front of me, two heads, tilted to the side, rested on each other, papers on the floor. Fortunately, no chance of a mishap because one guy's head was lodged firmly against the double-paned, hermetically-sealed window.

~

As our train pulled into the platform, the scene suddenly changed. Expressions remained blank. But the working warriors were now suiting up for their daily joust. Ties tightened and fixed, jackets placed on like coats of armor. Women tugged on their dresses to remove the wrinkles then checked their hair and makeup one last time.

The train screeched to a clumsy stop. A voice blared over the loud speaker, "Last stop, Grand Central Station." The train doors slid open; the warriors burst onto the platform. My imagination ran wild: I was sitting in a seat at the Roman Coliseum as the Christians were herded into the ring.

The train was now almost empty. I noticed a guy in an $800 Hugo Boss suit, rummaging from seat to seat. He picked up a crumpled copy of the *New York Times*, neatly folded and placed it in his attaché.

Chapter 23

$132,600 in Six Hours

JULY 1994

I was back from the brink of bankruptcy and working for a hot agency called Backer & Spielvogel located in the Chrysler Building on 43rd Street. The company's foundation was two mega accounts: Coca Cola Company and Miller Brewing Company. I had been appointed the senior management guy on the latter.

My administrative assistant, Marion Consuelo, had called in sick with a bad summer cold. The problem was I had a major presentation the next day at the Miller Brewing Company headquarters in Milwaukee. I needed help, and I needed it fast.

Fortunately, my human resources manager, Doreen Eickler, had an immediate fix. "You're in luck," she said, "I just interviewed an excellent executive assistant candidate for another Board member. I'm sure she would be happy to temp for a day or two until she finishes our interview process."

An hour later, an attractive dark-haired lady named Rosemarie introduced herself as my "temp for the day." She looked around. "Nice office. Bet you make a lot of money." We laughed.

I explained the timing of my meetings details and my travel preferences. "I'm not great at details, but I'm sure the other assistants will be happy to help if you have questions."

"No problem," she nodded. "I'm accustomed to finding solutions."

Before long Rosemarie had made airline reservations and developed a proposed itinerary neatly typed on two sheets of paper. It was perfect; I was impressed. She said, "Now, we just have to pay for the tickets and reservations." I explained our travel department had my personal stuff in their data bank. She replied, "I'm a temp, here for the day. Do you think they are going to share your personal information? Besides, suppose there's a problem, and we need to create a Plan B?"

Rosemarie was right. "Top right-hand draw, Marion made a folder with my credit cards and personal information," I replied. It's there if you need it."

I then dashed off to a prep meeting. When I returned the tickets were on my desk with a short-handwritten note. "Took care of everything. Marion's back tomorrow. Good luck. Rosemarie."

~

The meetings went well. We even got a new brand assignment. I decided to upgrade to first to congratulate myself. At the time, Backer executives only traveled first class on flights of more than four hours; New York to Milwaukee was less than three. I handed my AMEX card to the gate attendant, she made the ticket change then swiped my card. She shook her head, "I'm sorry sir, there must be a reader glitch, can I have another card?" I gave her my Visa Card. She looked at the machine. "Sir," she said starting to wonder, "the transaction is not approved."

I smiled and mumbled, "so much for letting my wife pay the bills." She glared, as if to say, "that wasn't a bit funny."

I took out a Diner's Club Card I said to myself, *this one's got to work, we rarely charge anything on it.* She swiped the card, the phone rang. She listened, nodded, and then handed me the phone. The voice on the other end said, "Hello, Mr. Crisci, this is the American Express Fraud Department." We then spent a few minutes validating who I was, then the voice said, "Mr. Crisci, transactional activity on all of your cards has been halted because of suspicious purchase activity."

"All my cards!" What the hell is going on?" I shouted. Everybody stared. The voice said, "I don't know, but that's a pretty drastic directive. I can connect you to…"

The people on line were annoyed, the clerk was brusque, "Sir, the plane leaves in 15 minutes. Can you or can't you pay for the ticket?" I took out an emergency check out of my wallet. I told the telephone voice, "I'll deal with the matter when I get to New York."

On the flight home, I had a couple of scotches, a nice dinner, and wondered what the hell was going on?

More bad news on arrival. As we drove home, Mary Ann assured me, "All our credit card bills are up to date. I'm not going through that embarrassment you created EVER again." When we were first married, I told Mary Ann, "me man, take care of money." Not soon after, I carried around several stamped envelopes for weeks — (this was before online banking). The dunning calls began. Mary Ann searched and found the envelopes. It took months to get our credit reports straight. I was never allowed to handle the bills again, and for the past forty we've never had another problem.

~

The next morning, I arrived at the office. There was no Marion, no Rosemarie. I called Doreen in human resources. "Strange, Rosemarie knew Marion was still sick, she said she'd be back today. Let me call her." A few minutes later, Doreen called back. "Rosemarie's phone just rings. I guess she doesn't have an answering machine."

"Doreen, I've got a bad feeling about this thing," I replied. "Can you check her address?" Doreen called back minutes later. "The police told me, the address she gave in the Bronx is actually an empty lot." I looked in Marion's drawer; my personal information folder was gone.

I picked up the phone and called American Express Fraud. The guy explained they would fax a summary of the charges run up in the six hours before they shut down activity. Visa and Diner's Club did the same thing. Minutes later, I was handed a series of faxes from each company. I look in horror. The total is $132,600!"

The charges were in three categories: long-distance calls all over the world; international electronic purchases; and women's clothing from shops around the city.

I called AMEX back. They assured me, "As a long-time customer, you are not liable for fraudulent charges. But the amount is a felony. We would advise you to file a police report, maybe they can track down the thieves." He also suggested I contact the other credit card companies to alert them and get new cards issued.

~

Next stop: the 17th Precinct on East 51st Street. The detective assigned to the case, Donald Dunn, looked at the fax charges. "These guys know what they're doing. They sold the cards to a long-distance middle man; the electronics in Singapore and Australia are untraceable and they probably unloaded the women's clothing to street merchants all over the City."

He paused and leaned back in his wooden chair. "So, what do you want me to do?"

"What do I want you to do? You're the police," I replied indignantly, "you're supposed to apprehend crooks."

"What did this Rosemarie look like?"

"She had long hair," I replied.

"What else can you tell me about her?"

I shrugged my shoulders.

"Sir," he replied calmly. "Do you realize if we chased every women with long hair around New York, we've have no resources left to deal with rapes, murders, robberies, and stuff like that?"

He glared. "What YOU might want to do in the future is not give all your personal information to somebody you know dick about! The best I can do is provide an official police report for your records."

"And what am I supposed to do with that?"

"You're going to need it," he replied. "When you start getting calls from the collection agencies about the phony retail store accounts they opened in your name."

"Detective," I asked, "What are you talking about?"

"Like I said, these guys were pros. As sure as we are sitting here, they also opened accounts at Macy's, Bloomingdales and places like that, and charged the shit out of them. Remember, you gave them your identity. So be prepared, once the 60-day grace period is over, you're going to be inundated with calls about charges you won't know a thing about. That police report will save your ass and your credit rating."

~

During the next six months, we received increasingly nasty dunning calls from Macy's, Bloomingdale's, Lord & Taylor, Loehmann's, Wanamaker's, Montgomery Ward, and Sears Catalogues. It took us six months to get store managements and their collection agencies to believe we weren't professional scam artists. And it took another six months to get our official records cleaned up, and our credit rating restored.

Chapter 24

Corner Table
at La Mela

APRIL 1995

I had just experienced an advertising executive's worst
nightmare — a happy client who proposed a media commission
reduction of 25 percent.

I decided I'd deliver the bad news to Chairman Phil Geier on a
full stomach. So, I'd trained it to Little Italy to enjoy some comfort
food — by myself.

As I climbed the steps of the Canal Street Station to the street,
the wind was howling off the East River. I buttoned my trench

coat and held my custom-made Worth & Worth hat tightly as I walked to Mulberry Street. About two blocks up Mulberry I spotted La Mela Ristorante. I looked in the window. It was nothing fancy and half-full; but it smelled like my grandmother's kitchen.

The friendly guy at the door lit up, "Welcome, welcome. So nice to see you." He sounded like my best friend. I started to walk to a window table. He pointed to a corner table in the rear of the restaurant, next to the open kitchen. "No, no. Better here. See everything."

I sat down and asked for a menu. "No menu," he said. "Just usual." Seconds later a liter of Chianti in a straw basket arrived with a mountain of crusty Italian bread and La Mela's interpretation of a caprese salad: chunks of fresh tomatoes mixed with chunks of fresh mozzarella. A hand generously poured olive and balsamic vinegar and ground fresh pepper. I finished almost half the dish. I was stuffed.

A large dish of lasagna arrived. The man placed two large sausages on the plate, "fresh salicia: one hot, one sweet, like always," he said. I forced myself to eat half of the entrée. I figured I'd skip coffee and dessert. "Good?" The man asked. "Prego," I replied, patting my enlarged stomach. I was about to ask for the check when he filled my wine glass and a 12-inch oval platter of chicken caccitori arrived. "Main course has our new sauce. Hope you like, better recipe."

After the caccitori came the cannolis and espresso. I was ready to be rolled out the door. All that remained was the check. I turned the bill over. It read $20.40. I knew there was a mistake. I pointed. The man smiled, "No, same like always."

I put my hat and trench coat on, the man followed me to the door. "Mario, say hello."

~

That night I sat in the living room reading the newspaper. There was a front page story about the mobster, Teflon John Gotti. He was standing next to his consigliere Bruce Cutler pleading with a judge. My mind flashed back three years before when I was mistaken as Cutler by a car full of Mafiosi.

I said to Mary Ann, "I think it happened again." She looked at me quizzically. "Remember when I told you about being mistaken for Bruce Cutler."

She laughed. "I love your stories."

I was insulted. "I thought we agreed after Tony and the Hubcaps, I didn't make up stories."

"Tell you what, " she said, "next time we go to Little Italy, I insist we eat at LaMela. I'd like to say hello to Mario."

~

On a cool and windy Saturday in early April, I suggested we spend the afternoon wandering around the SOHO galleries. She hadn't forgotten. "Only if we start with lunch at La Mela." To insure the same results, I decided to wear the same hat and trench coat. The cab pulled in front, she looked at the place, "This is where the famous Bruce Cutler eats. It looks like a dump."

We walked in, the place was packed. The woman at the door was taking names on a pad for the wait list. Mary Ann smelled the food. "It does smell good." She asked, "How long?" The woman replied, "No more than 45 minutes." Mary Ann looked at me. "There's a ton of good Italian restaurants within two blocks. Let's go find another one."

We started to open the door. Mario arrived. "Bongiorno, senor and senorina, your table ready in uno minuto."

I looked at the corner table. There was a young couple enjoying their meal. I had to make a bathroom stop. When I returned, the couple and their food had been moved to another table. And, my table had been reset with a fresh white table cloth, plates, silverware, basket of fresh bread, and an even bigger bottle of Chianti than the last time.

Mary Ann blinked her eyes, "What the hell just happened? I smiled like a cheshire cat. "Told you."

Mario and his team did a repeat of my previous meal. Like then, the stuff just arrived. We ate like pigs and readied to waddle out the door after we paid the check. It was $35.40. Mario and I looked at each other. "A little discount for the senorina. Tell John, treat all family the same."

I have told the LaMela story many times to many friends. They always have the same initial reaction, "Matt, you sure can tell a story." And Mary Ann always responds, "No, every word is true. I saw the whole thing with my own eyes."

Chapter 25

The Return of Meatloaf

FEBRUARY 1996

My niece Stephanie called about 6 PM to say she had two tickets to the Meatloaf Concert that evening at Madison Square Garden, but because of the heavy snowstorm she and her girlfriend didn't feel like going.

Stephanie knew I was a big Meatloaf fan ever since his first album, *Bat Out of Hell* went Platinum in 1977. (His real name was Marvin Aday from Dallas. He started as a night club bouncer). My first thought, "Thanks, but no thanks." I looked out the window and noticed the snow had stopped. "I'd love to, but it's so last minute.""

"Easy, uncle," said my problem-solving niece. "My girlfriend lives near the Garden, she can drop the tickets at the Will Call. The show starts at 8 PM, but you know rock concerts, that means 8:30, maybe later."

Mary Ann agreed. She knew how much I liked Meatloaf's music, and it was the first time he had performed in New York for quite a while. I called our concierge, Joe, to request a cab. Joe responded, "Sorry, Mr. Crisci, there just ain' any right now. Too much snow out there 'til the plows arrive."

"We'll walk," said Mary Ann. "It's less than a mile to the Garden."

Coats buttoned up, scarves wrapped around our necks, and black fur caps pulled tightly over our ears, we headed into the crisp, cold night air.

~

As we trudged over the pristine white snow dunes at a snail's pace, we were met by unfamiliar urban sounds — peace and tranquility; there were no planes, no trucks, and no police and fire sirens. The city of eight million had gone to sleep. About halfway, I started to wonder. If traveling 20 blocks was so difficult for, how in the world could Meatloaf, at the Grammy's in Los Angeles just 36 hours ago, make the trip? I offered Mary Ann a way out, "Suppose Meatloaf is a no-show because of the weather?"

"Ahhh," she remarked casually. "We've come this far, might as well find out. Worse case, no Meatloaf and we'll have to spend a night at one of those romantic little hideaways near the Garden."

About two blocks from the Garden, a large snowdrift came to life. The powdery white mound shuttered and a guy in tattered clothing with a leathery, potmarked face holding a whiskey bottle wrapped in a brown paper bag emerged from a large, brown cardboard box. The man looked at me with a big smile; his stained teeth filled with crowns.

"Hey buddy, can you spare a buck or two? Won't lie to you about needing something to eat." He waved the brown bag, "It's damn cold tonight and my heating fueling is running real low."

I started to wave him off; Mary Ann grabbed my arm. Her sympathetic eyes said, "Give the guy a break, at least he's being honest." Out came a $5 bill. Five dollars lighter seemed to make the last few blocks go faster. We turned the corner on 33rd Street and there was the Madison Garden marquee with hundreds of blinking lights, "Meatloaf Tonight." As we entered, the lobby was empty, there wasn't a soul on the Will Call line, and we were the only people on the escalators. I shrugged, "So much for the grit and determination of New Yorkers."

We got off the escalator and began looking for our section number. A courteous usher approached, "Let me show you to your seats. You've got some good ones, near center stage." He opened the curtain. I expected a half-empty Garden at best. The Garden lights were still up. We looked around, all 20,000 seats were filled! There were more smiling friendly faces than one sees in New York City in a week. It felt like a giant party waiting to happen.

~

The lights dimmed, exactly on time. The crowd chanted, "Meatloaf, Meatloaf." The bright curtain opened. A big hulk of man in a suit with a black cape, carrying a large red handkerchief walked on stage and addressed the audience.

"I want to thank you for coming," said Meatloaf. "I wasn't sure you'd make it because of the weather; and you probably thought the same about me. It took us about 31 hours to get here from L.A., but there was no way Meatloaf was going to be a no-show. I came to fulfill a promise I made a long time ago.

"As some of you may remember, the first *Bat Out of Hell* won four Grammys and sold millions of copies around the world." The crowd cheered. He smiled sanguinely, "But very few people know the story behind that so-called instant success. I traveled the country for 12 months begging disk jockey after disk jockey to play my music. I became quite familiar to rejection. One day I got a random call from Scott Muni at WNEW. He said, 'Meatloaf, your album is a bit off the wall, but this is New York, you never know.' Three months later, *Bat Out of Hell* was gold. The best part of the story is that 600,000 of the first million copies were sold in the Big Apple."

The crowd again cheered. Meatloaf wasn't finished.

"When Bat went gold, old Meatloaf made a promise. I would thank New York by playing my heart out at the greatest concert hall in the world before the greatest fans in the world."

The crowd stood and roared for what seemed like an eternity. Meatloaf looked around. We were close enough to see the tears in his eyes. "You know sometimes life don't go exactly as planned." He lowered his head. " I squandered the success you gave me. The drugs, the alcohol, I lost control. I became creatively bankrupt. Tonight, I'm happy to report, *Meatloaf has returned.*

"It's also been a lot easier to get *Bat Two* played this time around, but some things never change." He pointed to the crowd: "600,000 of the first million copies of *Bat Two* were again bought by the Big Apple. So think of tonight's concert as a thank you from Meatloaf's heart to your soul."

As Meatloaf walked off the stage, thousands of tiny bursts of light from matches and cigarette lighters filled the air. The curtain rose, the band began to rock, and Meatloaf roared onto the stage on his big black Harley motorcycle painted with red bats. First up: a soulful, seven-minute rendition of *I Would Do Anything for Love (But I won't do that)*. From there, Meatloaf and his band rocked with flair and theatricality; Madison Square Garden had been transformed into a celebratory Baptist Church welcoming the Lord.

~

Two hours later, the opening of the second set was as memorable as the first. Meatloaf again appeared alone, this time wearing an unhip checkered sports coat. A stew of reds, blues, white and greens that looked like a prop from the *Happy Days* television show.

"You're probably wondering why I'm wearing this sports coat. It's the first one I ever owned. As you can see, Meatloaf was a big boy, even at 15. But this coat kept me warm through some cold, dark moments. I'd like to introduce you to the man who gave me the coat, my father, Orvis."

A slight, ordinary man with a twinkle in his eye walked on stage and stood next to his son. It was hard to imagine, the mountain of a man called Meatloaf could be his offspring. "Dad traveled 31 hours with me to be here tonight. He wanted to thank you personally for your unwavering supporting of his son." The men hugged. Mr. Aday turned to the crowd, waved shyly and disappeared behind the curtain. Meatloaf's party resumed as people rocked, danced, and sang.

~

At 11 PM, as performers often do near the end of a concert, Meatloaf introduced his band and crew, and what appeared to be his lone backup singer in the shadows the entire evening.. "I want you all to meet Lorraine," he said, waving her to join him. "She's more than my lead vocalist, she's been my rock for more than 20 years. Without her, Meatloaf wouldn't be here tonight."

Meatloaf asked the audience, "Are you having a good time?" The crowd roared. "Glad to hear that because *we're going to play as long as you want to stay.*"

Meatloaf had one more announcement. "Before we continue I want you to meet Jim Steinman. He's Meatloaf's secret weapon — he wrote the music and lyrics and produced the arrangements for *Bat One* and *Bat Two*. To me, Jim has the strength of Goliath, the Heart of a Lion, and the krypton vision of Superman." A gleaming piano made of exotic hardwoods glided onto the stage. "This is where we make the magic," said Meatloaf. From behind the curtain, appeared a wisp of a man, at best five-feet five and 120 pounds, with long gray hair down to his waist. Steinman smiled and waved to the audience and sat down at the piano next to Meatloaf. The two men sat sang and played for the better part of another hour. When they finished, Steinman got up. The two men hugged. (Imagine Mutt and Jeff.) Steinman walked off stage. The crowd stood and applauded for three solid minutes.

~

Meatloaf now stood alone on the stage, openly crying. "I would like to say goodnight by singing what I believe is the greatest piece of music Jim ever penned, *Objects in the Mirror.*" When Meatloaf finished he waved and walked off the stage. Everyone in Madison Square Garden was emotionally spent. On the way out, people said little. They knew they had just witnessed a one-of-kind experience.

Chapter 26

Taxi Driver

SEPTEMBER 1998

What a great morning meeting!

Merrill Lynch had approved an increase of $20 million in next year's media budget, easily making them one of the agency's top three clients.

I looked at the clock next to Trinity Church at 75 Broadway. I had almost two hours before my midtown meeting at Bristol Myers Headquarters; just enough time for a power lunch at the Four Seasons Restaurant off Park and 52nd. I walked to the corner to hail a cab.

There were a number of empty Checkered Cabs with illuminated rooftop indicators. I was convinced this was my lucky day, so I decided to be a little picky. The first cab stopped. My prejudice showed. The driver was wearing a white turban. I waved him off. No interest in listening to an Arab talk to his friend on the phone while he figured out how to get me to my destination. (This was prior to the GPS explosion.) His eyes meet mine. He's slowed down, opened the window, started shouting profanities, and then slammed his foot on the gas.

Another cab — full of dents and dings from bumper to bumper — pulled alongside. I looked inside the passenger cabin; it reminded me of aftermath of the "Animal House" toga party. There were crumpled newspapers, empty water bottles, and a wad of pink bubble gum stuck to the divider. I shook my head; he went quietly.

Finally, a spacious Checkered Cab with a mirrored finish and gleaming chrome front and rear bumpers pulled up. Not only was the taxi driver a clean-shaven American, he was wearing a bow tie and white shirt. I got in, the cabin was immaculate.

"Good afternoon, sir, where to"? said the polite forty-something driver. "I'm Buddy."

"Four Seasons on 52nd Street."

"May I suggest we avoid traffic on the FDR — it's a nightmare around midday? We can just go straight up First Avenue." asked Buddy.

I smiled. "I'm in your hands."

~

As we pulled away, Buddy asked, "Ever been to Vietnam?" Odd first question, I thought to myself. "Can't say I have, why do you ask?" Almost immediately, my instinct told me it was the wrong question.

"Did two stints there, tank driver, 41st Infantry, Battalion C. I arrived a little naive like all the 20-year olds. First week in the field, my best friend Robby and I get caught in a fire fight in the middle of the dense jungle brush. After we called in some napalm, you could almost hear bodies toasting. Then there was silence. Our squad leader ordered us to bed down for the night, rather than struggle back to camp. Robby celebrated by walking to a clearing and taking a piss. On the way back, Robby stepped on a land mine. Never forget that scene. His body in was a bunch of bloody bits and pieces. I imagined Charlie laughing in some tunnel somewhere."

I really didn't know what to say. The taxi driver stared blankly, as he drove.

Suddenly, we were stuck in the middle of a big traffic jam created by a Con Edison crew repairing an underground cable. Between the crew, two trucks, rolls of cable, jackhammers and such, they had closed off three of the four lanes.

As we idled, Buddy had a flashback. I got to experience post traumatic syndrome upfront and personal. "Keep your head down, those fuckin' V.C. in that foxhole are armed to the gills. We'll surprise them from right." Suddenly, Buddy slammed on the gas pedal, drove on the sidewalk, and headed straight toward the manhole.

"These goddamn tanks are fantastic. They can go anywhere Charlie can go. When I get closer, drop a grenade into the foxhole; blow their little Asian asses off. They'll learn Buddy don't take no shit from nobody".

Terrified pedestrians scurried out of Buddy's way. I tried to bolt out the back, but Buddy had pressed the power lock. He paused for an instant, looking for the enemy; six Con Ed men in hard hats started pounding on the car. The more they pounded, the angrier Buddy became, "Don't worry pal, there's no way these bastards will capture us!"

Somehow Buddy threaded the needle, headed back onto First Avenue, and flew over the manhole cover with inches to spare. A fire truck siren began blaring few blocks away. "That's our guys to the rescue, like music to my ears. Bet we got them all, except for the one that tried to force his way into our tank."

~

I'm tried to stay calm despite my heart-racing 2,000 beats a minute. I was certain I was moments away from a massive cardiac arrest. I saw a group of patrolmen changing shifts, totally unaware of Buddy's rampage. I waved frantically and tried screaming through the closed window. They thought I'm waving to them. They waved back, as the rest of New York went about its business: jack hammers pounded away on the sidewalks, noisy garbage trucks and patrol cars made their rounds. At his point, Buddy — his white shirt now a mass of perspiration — became a calm stud — sort of. "Relax pal, you're in good hands. This is my second tour, no way those gooks can outsmart us."

We were now at 31st and First. The light turned red. Buddy slowed down and stopped like nothing ever happened. He turned and smiled, "Almost there sir, won't be long now. Right side or left? Near or far corner?"

~

I looked up First Avenue, the road seemed clear. About a block up, I saw a group of elementary school kids crossing the street with their teacher. They looked like a typical New York melting pot, black, white and Asian. Buddy spotted the kids, "Look there, crossing the open field, a whole platoon of unarmed Charlie. We'll run them down, crush 'em like ants." He stepped on the gas.

I started screaming, "Buddy, Buddy!" I pounded on the door, banged on the glass, trying to snap him out of his flashback.

"No sweat," he replied calmly. "I've got this one."

The teacher saw the cab hurling toward her group. She directed them to scatter between the parked cars or run into a few nearby stores. The sidewalk was now empty.

"Son of a bitch, what a time to run out of ammo. Let's get back to the base, tomorrow is another day, ya know what they say, "Killing a gook a day keeps the lieutenant away."

My heart was still pounding. Somehow, Buddy regained his composure. He stopped for the light at 44th Street, across from the United Nations. "Hey Buddy," I say calmly "it's hot as hell in here, mind taking the lock off, so I can open the window?"

"Sorry about that pal, the air conditioning broke earlier today," he responded pleasantly. "I didn't even realize the lock was on." The door lock popped open, and the window went down — not a moment too soon.

Buddy saw another taxi in front of him. To him, it was another tank blocking his path across some imaginary stream. "Get that God damn tank moving," he screamed, honking like crazy as the cab waited for the light to change. Suddenly Buddy stepped on the gas and rammed him in the rear. The furious driver headed straight for Buddy's window, "What the fuck! You crazy man?" He tried to tear open Buddy's door.

Buddy grabbed the clipboard off his seat, and started to swing viciously, like a machete slashing through dense jungle. "Fuckin' Charlie, this is for Robby!" The clipboard slit the driver's hand, blood splattered all over the dashboard, windshield and Buddy's pure white shirt.

I spotted two-armed security guards standing outside the UN Plaza Hotel, just 100 yards away. I bolted out of the car, attaché case in hand, and headed straight for the guards. Buddy saw me bolt, stopped slashing the other driver, jumped out of his car, a mass of blood and sweat, and started chasing me. "You killed my friend, you little shit, I'll cut your balls and hang them from a tree."

As I ran past the guards into the hotel lobby, I yelled, "Diplomat, the guy's crazy!" Trained for such matters, the guards tackled him high and low. Buddy had the strength of four men, the temper of six more. Ultimately, it took six guys to wrestle Buddy to the ground before they handcuffed and took him away.

As the crowds milled around, I noticed Buddy's car was still idling on the street, a symbol of what drugs and napalm and Charlie's indomitable spirit did to a whole generation of fine, young men. I had just witnessed, upfront and personal, what war can do to man's mind.

~

Suddenly, I was all alone in another time, memories swirled, like records on an old turntable. The turntable stopped. The year: 1962. It was 3 AM Friday night at the A&P supermarket on Gun Hill Road in the North Bronx where I worked nights to pay for college.

My night crew partner, Tony Cavallo, a big gentle, teddy bear of a man with crew-cut hair and arms spread wide like a B52 bomber, came flying down the aisle mimicking the sound of a large aircraft landing on the tarmac: gaaa, vroom, sssss!

Tony's plane came to a stop next to the smoked oysters! Tony loved smoked oysters. Typically, he would eat a whole can by himself, while his plane was being serviced for his next mission — stocking Tide, Ajax, Gain in the household cleaner aisle.

In time, Tony would graduate from Manhattan College, cum laude in engineering, and take a job with United Airlines as a commercial pilot trainee.

~

The turntable spun again: the year was 1986. My wife and kid were visiting the Washington Monument, the White House, and Lincoln and Jefferson memorials on our field trip to the nation's capital. The kids were tired and wanted to go back to the hotel. I insisted on one last site before we left: the Vietnam Memorial. I wanted to see names of the 41,000 young Americans who gave their life, chiseled in black granite, one by one. I knew Buddy's friend Robby was there somewhere.

As I scanned the monument, my eyes were drawn to the name Tony Cavallo. As I stood and stared, Tony's plane landed near the smoked oysters: gaaa, vroom, sssss!

Chapter 27

Pearls at Tiffany's

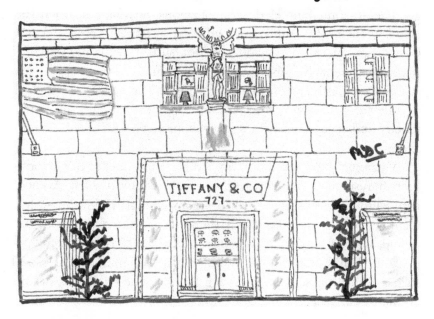

FEBRUARY 2000

Valentine's Day was fast approaching. After 36 years of marriage, I was looking for something different for my wife.

I opened the *New York Times*. There on page three was the answer. A Tiffany and Company advertisement suggested an elegant Elsa Petretti Sterling Silver Open Heart pendant and neck chain, "This simple, elegant, evocative shape celebrates the spirit of joy." At the bottom of the ad, in discreet, tiny type was the suggested price of $150.00 (including a 16" chain).

My mind flashed to Holly Golightly's fascination with the iconic Tiffany Building on Fifth Avenue *in Breakfast at Tiffany's*; my ears were filled with Henry Mancini's haunting *Moon River* melody. I imagined handing Mary Ann a little blue Tiffany box.

~

The next day around lunchtime, I entered Tiffany's front doors of the company's 727 Fifth Avenue flagship store. I didn't want the sophisticated sales staff behind the bronze-framed display cases to think I was a tourist, so I discretely asked the security guard just inside the door where the silver counters were located. He smiled, "Saw the ad, huh? In the rear to the left, sir."

The 40-something clerk was courteous, helpful, and when she heard it was a 36th Anniversary gift, she swooned. "How did you do it? I'm on my third, and still not sure." She completed the transaction, sent the tube upstairs, and pointed to the stairs to the gift wrap department on the second floor. Minutes later, I walked out the front door with my little blue bag, past counters displaying jewelry and accessories with minuscule price tags that read $25,000 and more.

Valentine's Day was a big win. An elegant dinner at our favorite French restaurant, Le Périgord, on 51st Street off First Avenue, with a little dessert surprise. I had organized a plan with the owner, Georgés Briquet, to place the Tiffany box on the tray next to the Grand Marnier Souffle. Mary Ann's eyes lit up. George's offered to place the bauble around Mary Ann's neck, "Ahhh, Monsieur Crisci such a romantic, must have French blood." The remainder of the evening went well at our apartment.

~

One Saturday a few months later, we were window shopping on Fifth Avenue. After leaving Bergdorf Goodman, Mary Ann spotted Tiffany's across the street. We decided to browse. I realized it was the first time she had actually been inside the store. She marveled at the 24-foot ceiling, the dark wood walls, and the well-lit display cases brimming with expensive suggestions.

We walked around for a few minutes. She stumbled upon display case with a variety of pearls. I spotted a string of large cultured pearls that were so big, I assumed they had to be costume jewelry. I whispered in Mary Ann's ear, "Can you believe it, Tiffany sells costume jewelry?"

"What are you talking about? "she replied. I walked over to the case and pointed to the price tag which *appeared* to read $250. A well-groomed sales associate appeared. She spotted the Petretti heart around Mary Ann's neck. "Always nice to see a client. I couldn't help but notice you looking at our featured strand of natural pearls. Would you like to try them on?"

"Featured strand?" I started to wonder about the price tag but remained expressionless. The sales associate continued, "The strand is truly one-of-a-kind. The manager calls it 'The Magnificent 38,' it's a precise duplicate of the Tiffany strand featured at the 1893 World Exposition in Chicago."

I realized I had made a BIG mistake!

"At $250,000 it may be the best buy on this entire floor," she continued. "You know, that strand 107 years ago was valued at $200,000."

Without missing a beat, Mary Ann responded, "They are lovely, and quite well-priced. The problem is that I have a small frame, and the pearls will look too pretentious. My friends might think I'm wearing costume jewelry."

Chapter 28

Sniffen Court

JULY 2001

About 10 PM, I was alone and not quite ready to go to sleep. It looked like a nice summer night, so I decided to go for a walk.

For some reason, I wanted to stop by the twinkling street lamps and tiny homes on Sniffen Court on 36th Street between Third and Lexington Avenues, a few blocks west of our East River apartment. Built in 1843 as paddocks for horses, Sniffen Court was named a historical landmark in the 1930's. Despite being in the middle of bustling midtown, the small homes had been lovingly maintained by a series of owners — a Big Apple oasis.

I had walked by the tiny street many times during the day, and even taken pictures. Sniffen Court at night was even more magical. The romantic natural slate stone street was dotted with homes with window boxes filled with colorful flowers and converted Nineteenth century gas lamps.

~

A hunched male figure in a long dark coat, black shoes, and a hint of gray hair protruding from a bowl-shaped hat, approached. His measured steps showed concern about an errant slip on cobblestones dotted with wet leaves from recent rains. The metal-tipped cane in his right hand, gently struck the cobblestones as he walked, creating a rhythm of sorts. Tap-tap.... tap-tap....tap-tap....tap-tap.

Our eyes met for a fleeting instant. Beneath the brim of the hat two thick, husky eyebrows and dark brown eyes stared into mine. I think, Jesus...I've frightened the bugger!

"Good evening sir," said the man.

"And good evening to you."

The man continued. "Just out for a little exercise before I turn in for the night. Sadie always said, 'you've always got to get a little exercise, no matter how old you are.' What about you? I know you don't live in the Court."

"How would you know that?" I asked.

"Lived here fifty years." He looked around at the buildings circling the Court. "Got here long before all the skyscrapers."

"Suppose I said I was the City's infamous cat burglar?" I joked.

He took a black-and-red-checkered handkerchief out of his pocket to clear his stuffed, pointed, round nose. "I'd say, you were the biggest cat burglar I ever saw."

We stood laughing.

"Sir... if you don't mind me asking, how old are you?"

"You first," he smiled.

"I'm almost 60."

"Oh, you're just a pup. I'm 89," he responded proudly. "Like to walk. Great walking city. Can't go as fast as I used to. Still like to do my own banking and shopping. Stop in the bank a few times a week to check my balances.... Actually, it's a good excuse to chat with the bank manager, Michele... She's real friendly. And, I get a free cup of coffee."

136

"You know, my mother does the same thing. Stop at the bank to check her balances and get a free cup of coffee." I said, "Maybe I should get the two of you together?"

"How old is she?"

"A spry 94."

"Well, she's a bit old for me. Never been involved with an older woman, not sure I should start at this stage of my life. What's her name?"

"Fanny."

"Pretty name. Is she a looker?"

"Not sure I can answer that, Sir. Beauty is in the eye of the beholder, as they say."

"Oh, you mean, she's your Mom and you're not sure what criteria *you* would use to answer *my* question."

"Yeah, something like that."

He put his hand out. "Call me Bennett, Son."

"Call me Matt, Bennett."

"Mom is a lot like you, Bennett. She looks forward to her walks. Fights to enjoy each day. She's in pretty good health and sharp as a tack…like you. She likes to visit friends in her senior citizens' apartment complex three, four times a day. She tells me a lot of them are too old to get around anymore."

"Does she wear eyeglasses? You know I don't wear glasses."

"No, Bennett, she doesn't wear glasses. The doctors say she has the vision of a 60-year-old."

"Does she cook?"

"She didn't cook very well when I was a kid! All I can say is she hasn't improved with age, if you get my drift."

"Sounds a little like my late wife, Sadie. I was an Appellate Court judge at Foley Square for many, many years. With my schedule, meals were always an erratic affair. We used to eat out a lot, long before it became fashionable, like today.

"Sadie and I had a wonderful social life, too. But most of all we shared a sense of passion for America; its values, its quality of life. We were born and raised in what is now Israel. Life was hard." Bennett shook his head a tiny bit as he continued. "The freedom people have in this country…the freedom people take for granted, was not so easy to come by in the old country. We learned very quickly in America, you fulfill all your dreams. There's only one requirement, you've got to be willing to work for them."

We walked slowly down the court.

"Sadie and I visited and revisited the unique landmarks that are so much a part of New York's history. Sadie's all-time favorite trip was riding past the Statue of Liberty on the Staten Island Ferry, and then looking at the Manhattan skyline as we returned to dock. She used to smile and say, 'Bennett, where else can you take a tour like this for nothing?'"

"Did Sadie like to take walks?"

"Oh yes...we used to walk everywhere together. She left the neighborhood about two years ago. But every now and then she comes back and walks by my side. We lived right over there...in number 13."

Bennett pointed to the last home by the gate with an oak tree and two modern residential towers in the background. "When we moved to Sniffen, that big oak tree was a lot smaller. Sometimes Sadie and I would sit in our garden for hours looking at the oak tree, just holding hands, not saying much."

Bennett picked up his cane and pointed. "There used to be a little Lebanese restaurant over there on 37th Street. Sadie loved the place. I can still hear, 'Bennett, order the tabbouleh, it's good for you.' He tapped his cane for emphasis. "Matt, ever had tabbouleh?

"Can't say I have, Bennett."

"It's really good...the parsley, the cracked wheat, lots of fiber. Sadie was such a wise woman. But things have a way of changing. I'm thinking of selling the place. Much too big for one person. I plan to move into a smaller place up the block with a doorman."

I was disappointed. "Bennett, this place is magical. Don't you want your kids to keep it in the family?"

"The only family left is my sister. Sadie was an only child, and we just never had any kids. I have a sister, Shiraz. But stayed in the old country. Never left. Still lives on the West Bank. She just celebrated her 104th birthday. Spoke to her the other day."

Naively, I blurted out, "The West Bank? Isn't that a little dangerous? Particularly at her age. I only know what I read in the paper, but why would she stay there?"

"Why…because it's her home, her roots. The West Bank is part of Shiraz's soul, just like America is part of mine." Bennett was so matter-of-fact, I felt like an idiot. "Matt, I am continually amazed why so few people in this country truly understand the power and importance of tradition, the notion of emotional roots." As we continued to walk and talk, I could not believe the depth of conversation I was having with an 89-year-old man I just met. "Ever think of becoming a judge?"

"No, Bennett, can't say I have."

"Taught me a lot about taking short cuts. Used to watch those fancy trial lawyers in my courtroom telling jurors, 'hey, while it's true my client may have falsified some books and records, maybe even made $30 or $40 million in the process, it's not like he murdered anybody.'"

"Yeah, I know what you mean, Bennett. I've seen some of those guys perform on television. They are clever, aren't they?"

His thick eyebrows stiffened as if somebody just sprayed them with laundry starch. "Clever! They're kind of pathetic. Got themselves so twisted, they're convinced wrong is right. Don't know diddley squat about values, about truth, about morality. I mean look at those shameless white-collar Bernie Brothers."

I thought Bennett was showing his age. There were no white-collar crooks called the Bernie Brothers. I chose to let things be.

He looked at me. "I know what you're thinking, there were no Bernie Brothers. Fact is those shameless bums, Madoff and Ebbers, were two of a kind. How could those guys even sleep at night, brothers or no brothers?" The more passionate Bennett became, the more erect he stood. His cane was no longer in use. "Why don't you come in, and have a cup of decaffeinated coffee?"

We sipped coffee in his jewel-box living room. "Sadie used to say, 'Bennett careful with the caffeine.' reminisced Bennett. "And, I would reply, Sadie, caffeine good for the mind."

For the next 45 minutes, I thought I'd taken a trip to the fountain of youth. He talked about race, foreign affairs, the economy, the new Mark Twain three-volume autobiography. I knew our chance meeting was something I would always cherish.

Bennett looked at his watch and smiled devilishly. "You're welcome to stay, but I'd like to catch the second half of *Dancing with the Stars?*"

I cracked up.

"What's so funny, don't you like that chick Pamela Anderson? Can you believe the body? I may be old, but I'm not dead yet!"

Bennett passed about two years later.

Every now and then, when I'm in New York, I stop by Sniffen Court, look at the big old oak tree, and imagine Sadie and Bennett holding hands in their backyard, not saying much.

Chapter 29

J.L.'s Christmas Tree

DECEMBER 2001

My overachieving son Mark arrived home with an an important announcement, "Dad, I made the basketball team."

I gave him a high five. "I'd like you to meet my teammate Jay. Coach Walsh said we'll be the starting backcourt. A nevous little black kid with curly hair walked in. "This is Jay Baines. We call him J.L. for short at school."

The boy's head bowed, eyes looking down. I smiled and reached out my hand, "Nice to meet you, J.L. You guys hungry? I always used to be famished after practice."

"Niccce toto meet you, Mr. Crisci. His gentle stutter now apparent. They were quite the pair. Mark at five feet, nine inches — about normal for a 16-year old — and Jay, probably no more than five feet, three inches. I thought to myself, what the hell kind of basketball team is this? A starting backcourt with a slow white guy who can't jump and a little kid with hands so small he probably can't get them around the ball.

As we sat and ate, Mark asked a question, "So, Pops (my nickname) how was your Saturday?

"Pretty nothing," I replied. "Your brother Matt hung little Mitch from the top of the freezer door in his Osh Kos overalls." And, when Mom got him down, Mitch came after me with your baseball bat because he said, 'I *always* let Matt do whatever he wants.'"

Jay, horrified, put down his glass of milk. "Whoooos is MMMitch?"

"Oh, he's Mark's three-year-old brother."

Jay attempted an awkward joke. "You know, Mr. Crisci, black people like me don't usually get invited into the fine homes of white people like you. Did you hang all your kids on freezer doors?"

I found Jay's attempt at humor demeaning. "Jay, you need to understand something, "I said warmly, "in this house you're Mark's friend. Understand what I'm saying?"

"I do, sir." The subject never came up again.

I learned something else during that snack. Mark was no longer Mark. Because of his rather pronounced nose, his teammates nicknamed him "The Beak." He loved it.

~

To my amazement, J.L. and The Beak put that high school team on their shoulders, and against all odds, willed their team to wins against teams they had no business beating. I used to sit behind the bench and listen to the huddle during timeouts. When things looked bleak, they would insist nothing was impossible. Often, they would go back on the court and prove it.

When they weren't playing a game or practicing with the team. Jay would take Mark down to the West Side to play on the asphalt courts with the more talented but less privileged. The first time I drove them, I couldn't help but notice he was the only white kid on the court and I was the only white spectator on the benches. I recalled my similar childhood basketball experiences in the South

Bronx. Despite that experience I got nervous when the slow white kid starting shouting instructions to his pickup teammates.

Quickly, Mark blew by two black kids and sunk a layup. They guarded him more tightly the next time down the court. He made a jump shot over their heads, then stole the next inbounds pass for another easy layup.

Jay laughed, so all the brothers could hear him. "Beak plays pretty well for a honky!"

I never again worried about Mark playing on the West Side. As he said, "playing with the best only make you better."

~

On weekends Jay would spend time at the house. I watched them go from teammates to best friends to brothers. Along the way they graduated from drinking cokes and playing video games to drinking beer and chasing broads. Somewhere along the way, they found time to play football. Jay was the unquestioned offensive and defensive star of the team, making every all-state team. Mark was an above-average blocking back, who occasionally carried the ball, and was a hard-hitting defensive back. When high school was over, they went different directions in college. Jay had a full scholarship to tiny Graceland in Iowa, while Mark passed up free basketball rides to play Division-3 three football at the academically elite University of San Diego.

By the end of sophomore year, Mark was flying high and loved his new environment. Jay did not adapt as easily. He returned home after his sophomore year, and never attended college again. Jay explained, "My grandmother, Mama Claire, was now alone since my grandfather passed. As the man of the house, I owed Grandma for raising me."

I've always believed there was a different explanation. Without his brother Mark by his side, Jay felt lost 2,000 miles from home.

The good news is that the boys made it a priority to stay in touch. Each Christmas, when Mark came home, it was like old times. They did everything together. One Christmas, we watched the lighting of the tree at Rockefeller Center on TV. Jay's eyes lit up when he saw the size and the thousands of lights.

"Jay, have you ever seen the tree at Rockefeller Center in person?"

"No sir, Mr. Crisci."

"It's settled then, Saturday we'll take the train from Stamford to Manhattan, see the tree at Rockefeller Center, make a visit to St. Patrick's Cathedral, and have a fun meal somewhere in the neighborhood."

"Is St. Patrick's one of those big Catholic Churches with all the statues of dead people? Never been in one of them."

Given Jay's limited experience outside of his hometown, I had another question. "Jay, have you ever had a pastrami and corned beef sandwich?"

"Is that one sandwich or two, Mr. Crisci. Doesn't really matter, I've never had either or both."

"Jay, Are you ever going to stop calling me Mr. Crisci?"

"No sir, Mr. Crisci.

~

The tree trip was quite a trip! The boys all took a bunch of pictures together. Jay's eyes popped when he saw the guilded cast bronze sculpture of Prometheus. "Who's that guy?" he asked.

"I figured I was spending about $40,000 per year on college for my two oldest sons, "Boys, will one of you explain the mythology behind Prometheus to Jay." They both stared blankly.

I decided to ask something simpler. "You guys hungry?" Everybody nodded.

"Let's walk over to Broadway, show Jay the Great White Way, then get some mile-highs at Jerry's Deli across from the Carnegie.

Mary Ann asked, "Why not the Carnegie?"

"Because real New Yorkers know the Carnegie is a tourist ripoff. You can get the same sandwiches across the street at Jerry's for half the price, and the meat tastes better."

Soon we were at the entrance to Jerry's. Jay, who was standing behind the rest of us, walked up to the hostess. "M'am, could you tell me.

Denise, the hostess, stared condescendingly at Jay and said, "I'm sorry, sir, our bathrooms are only for customers."

I was furious. "Jay's with us!"

Denise responded, "I'm so sorry. I didn't know."

"No, you're not," I replied bitterly.

Jay, not wanting to cause a scene, interrupted. "Mr. Crisci, it's alright. *They* don't mean anything by it.

After we were seated, I asked to see the manager. He and I stepped aside. I explained what happened. He tried to give me some bullshit that this stuff happens in New York. I waved my arms, "That's a load of crap. This is the 21st Century."

When I returned, Mark smiled, "Gave 'em hell, huh Dad," he said proudly.

After we finished a mountain of deli sandwiches, potato salad, kosher pickles and celery soda, I asked for the check. The manager returned. "The meal's on us."

~

Twenty years later. J.L. and The Beak remain best friends. J.L. is now considered part of the Crisci family. Beak made J.L. one of his best men at his wedding. Beak's children, Tino and Bella, call J.L. "guy" when he comes to visit. Nobody knows why. J.L. has one son, Zake, who will be graduating with honors from college soon. The Beak is Zake's Godfather, and plans to be at the graduation ceremony. Zake grew to be a bit taller than his Dad; he's six-foot six-inches tall!

Chapter 30

Scrambled Eggs, Strawberry Shortcake, and Mr. Kelly

DECEMBER 2003

After passing the shabby-looking TNT luncheonette on Eleventh Avenue for a decade, I decided to find out what kept the place in business.

As I entered the long, narrow shop, bacon was crisping on the grill, bagels popped in the toaster, and the aroma of acidic coffee hung in the air. I sat on an oil-cloth covered stool at the counter.

"Need a menu?" asked a weathered 40-something blonde, spatula in hand.

"What do you suggest?"

She stared, annoyed. "You ain't a regular, so how would I know what rings your chimes?"

"Why are you so sure I'm not?

"You've got this big peaceful smile on your face," she said. "Most of my regulars have some kind of a problem. Am I right or what, Carmina?" said the blonde looking down the gray Formica counter at the disinterested waitress — an ungroomed woman in her late 20's with long black hair and a flawless olive complexion."

"No lie," said Carmina.

"Carmina, will ya put the paper down and take the man's order," chided Theresa, "Don't wanna give this guy the impression we ain't got no class."

"So, what'll you have, sir?" asked Carmina, pencil in her ear.

"Eggs over, rye toast, side of sausage."

"Thought so," she said. Carmina winked, then shouted at Theresa standing by the griddle, five feet away, "two bullets over, whiskey side, pigs legs." I watched Theresa as she cooked: earthy, interesting, intentionally unkept, a slightly wrinkled complexion and two jewel-like blue eyes. "Kinda figured you'd order the daily special," she said. "What do you do that makes you walk around with that big smile?"

"I'm a writer."

"What kind of writer?"

"I write stories about people and their experiences, as they wander through the ups and downs of everyday life."

"Sounds depressing. Did you have an unhappy childhood, or something?" she asked.

"Why do you think every day experiences have to be depressing?"
She walked back to the griddle and started to make another stack of home fries.

"I believe we all have experiences to share. Experiences that can be personally cathartic and maybe, just maybe, provide a kind of comfort to others, because they discover they're not alone."

She stopped turning the fries, put her spatula down, wiped her hands on a rag, turned and walked over. "You really believe that?" I nodded. She stuck her hand out. "Hi, I'm Theresa. What's your name, writer?"

"Matt."

She laughed. "You mean, Matt like in a rug?"

I laughed. "Theresa, my instinct tells me TNT is a warehouse of stories."

"You want stories? Boy, could I tell you stories. They spill their guts at TNT. Sometimes, I think I'm a goddamn shrink!" Theresa walked down the counter. "Carmina, do we hear stories or what?"

"No lie, Theresa. Remember Louie Spaghetti and the Meatballs?"

"Theresa," I said, "you're not going to leave me hanging by the meatballs?"

"We've got this customer, Louie. Don't know what his last name is. Never asked. He's married 35, maybe 40 years. Good-looking guy for his age. He comes in here every Thursday, orders my spaghetti and meatballs. Sometimes he orders meatballs and spaghetti." She paused. "Get my drift? Carmina and I named him Louie Spaghetti and the Meatballs."

Carmina said, "Theresa, why don't you tell writer man about Mr. Kelly. Theresa took a deep breath. Her expression changed. "Mr. Kelly...if you had the time...now that's a story!"

"I've got time," I said.

"About five years ago, this well-mannered, gray-haired gentleman walked into my restaurant and ordered scrambled eggs, cooked firm, with a side order of strawberry cheesecake. Then he started to show up every second or third day at 11:15 AM. We got to talking. Nothing heavy. Eventually, he came in every day. Always ordered the same damn thing. He told me he was a retired prison guard from Rikers Island. Nice old guy, a bit shy, tended to keep to himself as he sat at the counter. Smoked a pipe.

"It took about six months before he formally introduced himself. Told me his name was Richard Kelly. Had lived in the neighborhood for almost 17 years. Rented a little apartment over a laundromat. Didn't drive or own a car. I became fond of the old guy. In a strange way, we became luncheonette buddies."

Theresa's face turned sullen. "About two years ago, he began to get a growth on his lips. At first, we thought it was a fever sore, or maybe a reaction to his less than stellar diet. Like how many scrambled eggs and how much strawberry cheesecake can one man eat?"

"Anyway, the growth got larger. I told him he should go to the doctor. Mr. Kelly told me, he didn't have a doctor or even any medical insurance. I suggested we visit my doctor. I told him not to worry about the money thing, I'd pay for the visit. I just wanted him to get better. He refused. I kept asking. He kept refusing." She continued, "Eventually, the growth got so large, he could no longer speak. But every morning at 11:15, he arrived with an order for scrambled eggs, cooked firm, and a side of strawberry cheesecake, scribbled on a piece of paper. The sore got larger and uglier. He grew increasingly self-conscious. When he ate, he kept his head down, so people wouldn't see the sore. I begged him to let me help. Eventually, the growth covered his entire mouth. He wouldn't come into the store anymore; he was too embarrassed."

~

Mt stomach got queasy. "What happened?"

"Time went by, it was a scorching, hot summer day. I hadn't seen Mr. Kelly in weeks. Suddenly, he wobbled in — looked really, really weak. Must have lost 70 pounds. I almost cried when I saw him. I made him the usual. Put it in a brown bag. He took the order and started walking across the street. As I looked out the luncheonette window, I could see he was stumbling and swerving, desperately trying to hold onto that bag of food. He grabbed onto the lamppost. I wept like a child."

Theresa stared out the window, as she relived the moment. "Right there and then I decided I couldn't let him be any longer. I closed down the luncheonette and went straight to the social services office. Told them the whole story. They said politely they had a very busy schedule but would check into the situation in about five days. I wigged out. "That's not good enough," I screamed! I refused to leave until I spoke to a supervisor. Fortunately, the supervisor was very understanding. She agreed to send someone over to his house the following day. Just give us Mr. Kelly's address, she said, we'll take it from there.

"I realized, I didn't even know his address. Told the supervisor I'd get the address, and phone it in by noon. Just make sure the social worker who will be dealing with the case is available."

"How did you expect to get the address?"

"Woman's intuition," responded Theresa. "Sure enough, Mr. Kelly showed up at the usual time for his usual order. That's when I put my little plan into action. I told him the griddle was broken, and that I was waiting for the repairman. He headed back to his apartment. I followed him, like a private detective. After he went into his building, I took out my cell phone and called the social worker. I told her I was going to camp out across the street to make sure he didn't wander off before she arrived.

"The social worker arrived in less than 15 minutes. We rang the bell in the lobby. He didn't answer. I began shouting his name outside the building. Neighbors poked their heads out their windows wondering what the hell was going on. Mr. Kelly finally peeked out the window from a second story apartment. He waved us away. We persisted, demanded he let us in…but to no avail."

~

A large tear formed in the corner of Theresa's eye and slide down her cheek. She walked back to the grill, like I didn't exist. "

"What happened to Mr. Kelly?" I asked.

"I can't talk about it anymore."

"Theresa, please."

She stared silently for a while. Then acquiesced. "What the hell, why not. Might be good for me to finally let it out." I gave her a gentle prompt. "He refused to let you in…"

"Yeah, yeah, like I was saying, the social worker was really frustrated–almost angry–because Mr. Kelly wouldn't open the door. I'm crying like a baby, right on the street. The social worker made one last effort. 'Mr. Kelly, if you don't open the door, you will leave me no alternative but to call the police and have them force their way in.'

The second-floor window slowly creaked open. 'No, no, please don't call the police,' he begged, 'I'll let you in.' Mr. Kelly staggered down the stairs and opened the door. I said, 'Mr. Kelly, please don't be mad at me, I just want to help you.'"

He replied, voice strained, 'I'm not mad, I understand.' That was about all he could say. The rest of the time we communicated in writing and home-made sign language. Basically, he agreed to go to the hospital for an examination. But, he scribbled, he couldn't go for a few days because he had a number of personal matters to take care of. 'I can't leave my apartment. My landlord doesn't give a shit!' I had no idea what the hell he was talking about.

"By now the local police had spotted the commotion and entered the house. After listening to the social worker, they told Mr. Kelly either he went to the hospital voluntarily or they would handcuff him and drag him there in the police car, 'Mac, somebody has got to look at your mouth, it's disgusting!' Defiantly, Mr. Kelly stuck out his hands as if to say, 'Go ahead, I dare you… handcuff me!'"

Theresa's eyes were filled with tears.

"Sobbing, I reached out, took his hands and placed them in mine. I told the cops to leave him be, I'll take him to the hospital. Mr. Kelly smiled. Off we went off to the hospital arm and arm."

~

"I got a call at the luncheonette the next day from a lady with a deep voice. She said she was Mr. Kelly's sister. The landlord called her to let her know he had been evicted, and she had thrown all of his personal belongings in the garbage. I was incredulous. She blamed me. 'Goddamn you, lady!' she screamed into the phone, 'Who the hell are you to butt into my brother's affairs?' She slammed the phone in my ear — I never even got her name. I closed the luncheonette and went to the police station to explain the situation. 'His rent is current. I paid it myself,' I cried. Mr. Kelly has rights; he's a human being. The police were completely unsympathetic. They said in this state, a landlord could evict Mr. Kelly and his belongings at will, if they so choose.

"That night around eleven I went to Mr. Kelly's home. Searched the garbage outside for his belongings. I called the landlord and told her what she was doing was not right, not humane. If she didn't put his stuff somewhere until he returned from the hospital, I would give the whole story to the local newspaper and embarrass her to death!

"The next day the landlord came to my restaurant and told me she was going to have me arrested for trespassing. She wouldn't leave. Carmina called the cops. The landlord had to be forcibly removed from my luncheonette and warned by the police to never set foot in my place again or she would be arrested for personal harassment. The next day I walked by Mr. Kelly's place. The landlord had put a *No Trespassing* sign on the property.

"I went to visit Mr. Kelly at the hospital but didn't dare tell him about what was going on. I figured he already had all he could handle — the doctors at the hospital still hadn't figured out what he had, much less how to treat it. A few days later, Mr. Kelly was moved from our local hospital in Port Chester to the experimental treatment unit at Westchester County Medical Center, for more detailed tests and further observation.

"For the next week or so, I went back and forth visiting him twice a day. On the morning run, I always brought him an order of firm scrambled eggs and strawberry cheesecake. Finally, the doctors declared he had a rare form of jaw cancer with some complicated name. They told me there were maybe two cases a year in the entire United States. The doctors explained to Mr. Kelly that he required a complicated 12-hour procedure where all the facial skin from the middle of his face down to his neck would be removed and replaced with skin from other parts of his body. I cringed in horror. The procedure sounded like pure torture.

"Mr. Kelly said no. I'm an old man, let me die. I tried to convince him otherwise because during this whole ordeal, I discovered he was only 69, and had a lot of living yet to do. He agreed, reluctantly. A few days before the procedure, he gave me power of attorney to act on his behalf for all matters pertaining to him. I felt like family. The responsibility made me feel good, in a sad sort of way.

"First thing I did was send a certified check to his landlord for the next month's rent. I wanted him to have a place to call home; I knew how important that was to him. The check came back a few days later with an attorney's letter saying Mr. Kelly no longer lived there. I was so busy taking care of his other matters; I figured I'd get to this issue during his recuperation period after the surgery. I thought it was more important to spend time with Mr. Kelly, rather than fight with the son-of-a-bitch landlord.

"The day of the operation, we were both nervous as hell. The doctors informed me this was an *experimental procedure*. Translation — I could watch the operation in the observation pavilion along with the other surgeons. I decided to do it. My dear God, it was absolutely unbelievable — first, they removed half his face. Then the doctors took two of his ribs and made them into jaws. His stomach skin became his cheeks. The cancer was everywhere. I stood on my feet almost twelve hours. I cried about ten of those hours. I could feel his pain."

Theresa's description of the surgery left me shaking.

~

"After the procedure, his head was wrapped like a mummy for days. But he was talking again through the tiny slits in the front of the head dressing. No more handwritten notes. He kept talking about going home. I didn't have the heart to tell him he had been evicted.

"When I got home, I called the Office of Social Services. The caseworker and I were now on a first-name basis. She said she'd meet with Mr. Kelly to discuss his options. I felt obligated to be there. After she broke the news, Mr. Kelly asked me to read the note from his landlord. He cried and cried.

"He begged me to write some letters for him, plead his case to anyone who would listen. The landlord, the lawyer, the police, the city. I agreed. I spent the next three evenings composing and typing notes. A week went by. There was absolutely no response from anyone.

"I went to see the landlord myself. Told her how upset Mr. Kelly was, what he had been through. The landlord paid a visit to Mr. Kelly. I don't know what she said, but when I arrived, Mr. Kelly was beside himself. He was hyperventilating. I instructed the hospital staff to bar the bitch from ever visiting Mr. Kelly again. Mr. Kelly was in the hospital, same room, same bed for three months. His mail was now being forwarded to my luncheonette. His life was now mine.

"Apparently, some of his mail slipped through the cracks, accidentally went to his old address. One day the landlord stormed into my luncheonette. She said, 'Here's your mail!' then threw the pile at me. As I picked the stuff off the floor, she started verbally abusing me. 'Listen bitch, butt out. Kelly's affairs are none of your goddamn business!' She kept going. I had to call the police. My customers were horrified. Half of them fled, and half of them wanted to beat the shit out of her."

~

"The whole thing had become too much. I needed a break. I decided to go on a little three-day vacation, first time in five years. Went to the hospital to tell Mr. Kelly I wouldn't be visiting for a few days. I was so frightened what his reaction might be, I asked my mom to come along with me for moral support. 'I'm going on a little vacation, Mr. Kelly,' I said cheerfully. 'But don't worry, I'll call you while I'm away.' The doctors took me aside to discuss next steps — like I was next of kin. They explained the surgery had gone well, and that they wanted to begin the slow, and somewhat painful, procedure to restore normative facial functions. When I returned to the room, the medical team had just removed the gauze from his face. The upper portion around his eyes and forehead were beet red, the lower portion looked like a smooth plastic block. It was horrible. I just held my mom's hand very tight, bit my lips and cried inside.

"He was in such pain, he was unable to speak and unable to write. It was simply not the time to discuss what I had just been told. I went outside and cried, 'Mama, with all this man has been through, it's just not right. Why, Mama? Why?'

"I decided to discuss the matter with the doctors. Nonstop questions: Can you do something for his pain? Is all the additional surgery necessary? I'm politely told I'm challenging their professional judgment. They do a complete 180. 'Madam,' they say arrogantly, 'we really shouldn't be discussing Mr. Kelly's condition with you any further. This is a private matter for immediate family.'

"By the time I left the hospital it was 6 PM; I was emotionally spent. I packed my bag for my trip and then collapsed in bed exhausted. The next thing I know, the sun is streaming through the window, and, the phone is ringing. I look at the clock; it's 9 AM. I'm amazed. I never sleep that late. It was the hospital. They told me Mr. Kelly died about 8 PM the night before. They wanted my approval for an autopsy. Said it would be valuable for future cases.

"I think to myself, those bastards wouldn't discuss his condition because I wasn't family, but they find me to get my approval to dissect and cut him up the sake of medical research! I told them, absolutely not! I decided it was time to go through all the personal papers he left with me, maybe I could find some clues to his life. Turned out he was married twice, and both his parents were cremated."

"I also discovered he had a cousin who lived nearby. I called her to explain that he had just died. She came over to my luncheonette when I got back from the trip. She rifled through all his papers and letters — like she was looking for a pot of gold. Never said thank you; never asked about his ordeal. All she volunteered was that Mr. Kelly had a brother named Gene Willis in El Paso, Texas. 'You might want to call him,' she said, and then left.

"Got the brother's number through information. I called and asked the voice on the other end of the phone said, 'Yeah, I had a brother named Richard, but I haven't spoken to him in 17 years.' I told him his brother just died. The guy responded, 'Was he happy at the end? Did he have a good life?' What could I say?

"Then he asked, who I was. 'How did you know my brother?'"

"I explained to the voice I was sort of his soul-sister these past five years. Thought he was all alone. Didn't know he had a brother, until I went through his papers, found a cousin, who referred me to you.

"Have you talked to his son and daughter?" asked the voice. I was stunned he had children. There was absolutely nothing in his personal papers.

~

"Next day, I called the son. Got his wife. Explained the whole thing. Mentioned I could use a little financial help with the burial and other arrangements. Never heard back. Called one more time. Nothing. I received a call from the hospital. They informed me they had received a call from somebody who identified himself as Mr. Kelly's son. Wouldn't give a phone number or address, just said he didn't want the remains. Told them to do whatever the hell they wanted with the body. The morgue also called to inform me that his sister visited his slab, went through all his belongings, then just left."

Theresa sighed. "Mr. Kelly. The man nobody seemed to care about." There was more... "I called my brother, who had a funeral parlor on 116th Street. He was kind enough to help me make some simple arrangements. At least provide Mr. Kelly a little dignity in death. My brother also ran a little funeral notice, as is the custom."

Theresa walked over to the cash register, lifted the tray, pulled out the funeral notice and placed it on the counter in front of me. "Believe it or not, while all this was going on, I was still trying to make a living running my luncheonette. A few days later, the phone rang. The voice said she was Mr. Kelly's daughter. She started harassing me about his accounts, 'Where is all the goddamn money?' I told her I didn't have any idea what she was talking about. That I took money out of my own pocket to bury her father. She hung up in my face!

"Stupid me! Despite all the crap, I ran the notice and went ahead with a simple burial ceremony. Mr. Kelly's landlord showed up, so did his daughter. And there was a third person. The priest told me man had introduced himself as Mr. Kelly's son. Not one of them talked to me. They all just gave me dirty looks.... like I was some kind of leper. I felt filthy and unclean. It was so, so painful.

"My blood virtually at the boiling point, I began thinking to myself, *this is what took five years out of my life...five years out of my life*. At just that moment, a light switched on in my mind, my anger and frustration subsided. My eyes came to rest on the open casket where Mr. Kelly lay peacefully for the first time in a long, long time. My soulmate's journey had come to an end."

~

"I bowed my head and said a Hail Mary and an Our Father under my breath. When I raised my head, I was alone. I wondered, were the attendees real or a figment of my imagination? I decided it didn't matter."

Theresa smiled. "After I left the funeral I came back to the luncheonette and made an order of firm scrambled eggs and strawberry cheesecake, just the way Mr. Kelly liked it. I don't know why, I just did. I even put the stuff in a brown to-go bag, labeled it, *Mr. Kelly,* and placed it next to the grill. A few minutes later one of my regulars came in. I took their order. When I returned to the grill, the bag was gone. I knew Mr. Kelly stopped by to pick up the bag, so he wouldn't get hungry on the way to his new apartment."

I smiled and readied to leave. "Thanks for sharing, Theresa."

"See you, Writer. Hope you write a good story." She handed me a warm brown bag. Here's something for the road."

Chapter 31

$50 Prada Handbag

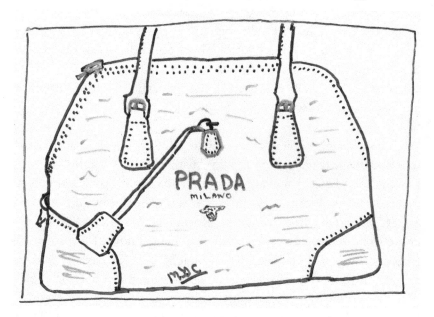

APRIL 2004

Everybody knows New York has incredible attractions like the Statue of Liberty, the Metropolitan Museum of Art, Greenwich Village, and Wall Street, to name just a few.

But there is a lesser-known and unique New York attraction that remains virtually unknown though it's ubiquitous and impervious to economic cycles. It's called the *Brand-Name Knockoff Industry;* it has operated as a cottage industry with relative impunity in multiple distribution channels for more than 50 years.

One of the industry's high-traffic locations has been Fifth Avenue between 49th Street and 59th Street. There, in full view of New York's Finest, industrious, entrepreneurial vendors with unlicensed portable stalls blatantly pitch their deals: "Why spend a ton at Bijan, Vuitton, Cartier and Fendi when you can buy a great-looking facsimile at a fraction of the cost?"

During the sixties, the knockoff vendors were mostly black. But that changed after the race riots in Newark and Watts. White European tourists — big buyers of knock-offs — heard stories of being harassed while shopping, so they avoided black vendors like the plague. Sales plunged.

Slowly but surely a new type of vendor evolved — white people with European accents. Their soft-sell made customers believe the junk merchandise wasn't junk. The European sound-alikes were also well-organized. Different stalls featured different lines of merchandise.

~

I first became a stall customer in 1976. Mary Ann and I had returned from three great years in Australia; and I wanted to look as worldly as I felt. I was attracted to Klaus Mayer's (who knows if that was his real name) Rolex watch stand in the middle of 53rd Street on Fifth, not far from Rockefeller Center. Klaus had attractively displayed some Rolex Day-Date knockoffs on a dark blue display board the size of his attaché case, in case he had to quickly close up shop. I picked one up; it looked just like the 1950's timeless classic and felt quite substantial. Klaus commented, "These are hard to come by. I only can get a few at a time. Trust me, you can't go wrong for $50 dollars. It will look great with your suit and tie."

As Klaus went for the close, his accent thickened. "These watches are not American-made, they are imported." Klaus looked around dramatically, "If you don't tell anybody, you can have for $40."

I headed back to my office with the fake-gold Rolex on my wrist. My assistant Janet said, "Boss, they're waiting for you in Conference Room C." She noticed the watch under the French cuffs on my shirt. "You must have gotten one hell of a bonus for that Australian gig. Don't forget to share the wealth."

During the next two weeks, I received so many compliments from my peers about the damn watch, I was convinced I was wearing the real thing — until that day. The client meeting was almost complete. There was just one creative concept left to present. The creative team sensed the client was losing focus. "Matt, how much time do we have left?"

I looked at my watch, the dials were frozen. Without missing a beat, I responded, "About 20 minutes."

That evening on the train heading home, I started banging the watch on the side to restart the mechanism. The guy next to be was horrified. "Jesus, do you always treat your Rolex like that?"

I tried to pry the back open. I discovered the case was glued shut. When I arrived home, I told Mary Ann I got ripped off. She laughed, "What did you expect for $40?" I vowed to never buy another knock-off anything. *Only a fool does exactly the same thing a second time, expecting a different outcome.*

~

On a beautiful spring evening in Manhattan 32 years later, we had just finished a romantic candlelight dinner at our favorite restaurant in Little Italy — Il Cortile on Mulberry Street. Mary Ann always laughed when I ordered the off-the-menu specialty: "Seni di Venere" (Breasts of Venus), two hand-pounded pieces of veal with a giant dollop of sautéed spinach on top, covered with a whole fresh mozzarella, and baked in the oven till each piece looks like a giant breast. A black olive is put in the appropriate place on the breast, and each breast is covered in a light delicate, lemon flavored brown sauce.

We decided to walk down to Canal Street, then maybe cross the Brooklyn Bridge. We got no further than the corner when Mary Ann spotted a knockoff store with Fendi, Gucci and Louis Vuitton pocketbooks displayed in a large picture window. She stopped. I shook my head, "Junk."

She responded, "They don't look bad to me." A Chinese women came out of the store. "Lady want bag? Nice brands. Good quality." I shook my head, no. The women persisted. Annoyed, I blurted out, "Look at my wife, does she look like someone who'd carry a knockoff?"

The woman stared at Mary Ann. "Pretty lady. Nice dress. Wrong bag."

The woman convinced Mary Ann to visit the rear of her shop where she kept "the best bags for best customers." Mary Ann decided to take a peak. I waited outside. Five minutes went by, then ten. Mary Ann walked out holding a red Prada Leather bag.

"She got you," I said sarcastically.

"You're wrong, this looks and feels exactly like the Prada bag I saw in their Fifth Avenue store for $3,500." I said nothing. Mary Ann was happy and that was all that mattered.

A few weeks later, Mary Ann joined me on a business trip to Los Angeles. We decided to window shop on Rodeo Drive. Mary Ann looked her usual casually elegant self with the Prada bag in hand. I tagged along, concerned the window shopping should have *some* reasonable financial parameters. We entered Jimmy Choo. She walked over to the display rack and picked up a pair of Lilian 100 Suede pumps. The price tag read $1,650. Mary Ann gulped. A sales advisor approached. "Madame, those shoes would look great with your outfit."

Mary Ann replied, "$1,650 is more than I wanted to spend for a pair of shoes."

The adviser became a tad truculent. "Madame, tell me something, how does one justify $3,500 for a *nice* Prada bag, but finds the *best* shoes in the world too expensive?"

Chapter 32

Village Magic

FEBRUARY 2006

The sun was bright and the sky a bright blue when the town car left Newark Airport and headed for our Midtown apartment.

"Thought there was supposed to be a big snow storm," I remarked to the driver. "It's the main reason we cut our San Francisco trip short."

"It's coming," he replied.

"Why are you so sure?" I asked.

"Over there, see, the Meadowlands, where those birds live." A body of water near Giants Stadium in New Jersey, minutes from Manhattan, with an unusual ecosystem that supports four species of waterfowl. He slowed down and pointed. The cars in the rear came to a stretching halt and started beeping. The driver remained oblivious.

"When they ain't here, it snows. And, there ain't a one."

Back in our apartment, we were drinking a glass of wine and listening to Billie Holiday when the snow started falling and the skyline slowly turned white. By morning the snowfall had become the city's largest in decades — 24 inches in Central Park. New York had been transformed into a pristine Rockwellian urban landscape — no cars, no pedestrians, no frenetic horns, no police or fire sirens.

Somehow, the *New York Times* had still made its way to our door. We sat and read against a backdrop that featured the art deco dome of the Chrysler Building and the tilted triangular Citicorp headquarters glistening in the bright sun.

Mary Ann — a passionate gourmand who planned to eat at every well-reviewed restaurant in New York before heading to the heavenly Wolfgang Puck's Spago in the sky — said, "Look at this review, the place sounds yummy."

Osteria del Sole was an Italian-Mediterranean bistro on 4th and Perry in the West Village. According to the write-up, it served homemade cuisine, had a romantic atmosphere, an attentive staff, and fair prices — a rare combination in New York. "Let's skip breakfast and have an early lunch," she said.

I suggested the place might not be opened because of the storm. But Mary Ann was on a mission. "I'll call in a while to see if they plan to open." Soon, she returned. "I just talked to Sylvester, he said, 'Come anytime. No busy today.' If Sylvester suggested we come, I propose go." I had no idea who the hell Sylvester was.

"The city looks deserted," I said. "I don't think we're going to find a cab."

"We can take the subway. Osteria looks like it's only a few blocks from the station." Evidently, we were going no matter what because Mary Ann never rides the subway.

~

The six-block walk to the Lexington Avenue subway was exhilarating but challenging. The snow was 24-36 inches in spots, and the street corners were like navigating moguls on a ski slope. In all my years, I had never seen New York's streets and sidewalks so clean and white. In spots, ours were the only footprints.

At first blush, life inside the subway station seemed business as usual. The trains rumbled back and forth, a sullen toll operator sat motionless behind her clear bullet-proof window, and the newsstand was open. The only thing missing: people. We were the only riders on the platform, and when we arrived at Washington Square's West Fourth Street station, the only people on the street.

As we trudged up West Fourth, we saw a weathered brick four-story orange building in the distance on Perry Street with a brightly colored corner awning that read simply "Osteria del Sole." The owners had cleared the street in front of the place and piled all the snow at the edge of the sidewalk.

Inside felt like a jewel-box for adults. The green and gray pastel walls were dotted with dimly lit, hand-hammered copper lanterns, and the 15 empty tables were decorated with fresh flowers. In front sat an oversized antique mahogany bar with a brightly-lit Mediterranean sun above the bottles and glasses. On the corner of the bar sat an old mechanical adding machine, wedged between two jeroboams of Italian red wine.

A man of average height and build with a head of unruly black curly hair greeted us with a big smile. "You must be Senorina Mary Ann. I'm Sylvester. Usually host; today host and cleanup." He seated us in the window and brought menus. "Want to hear the specials?" asked Sylvester. "No," I responded, just bring what you like we eat everything." Mary Ann frowned. She has never liked me doing that.

He poured a light, fruity red wine into our glasses. He walked to the bar, returned with another glass and said, "Okay I join you?" That was a first for us. "I have selected what I would eat. Hugo (the chef) will take his time, no rush, eh?"

We smiled. We soon discovered Sylvester and Hugo met and fell in love five years ago in Southern Italy, not far from where Mary Ann's mother was born.

The first course was baked, breaded calamari so tender they melted in your mouth. "Little secret," said Sylvester. He returned with a clove of garlic and a cheese grater. "Sprinkle brings out Hugo's flavor."

Another bottle of wine and a *secondi* course. More conversation, more laughs. And so the afternoon went. Three bottles of wine, four courses of food.

As we headed for the homemade cannoli and espresso, Hugo joined us. "Sylvester tells me you are lovely people. Married, what, 42 years?"

Hugo looked at the table. "Where's the champagne? We must celebrate." Sylvester popped the cork; it pinged off one of the lanterns. The light went out. We finished the entire bottle. I ended with my customary grappa digestive. Mary Ann looked at her watch. It was about 4:30 PM. "Oh my God!" she said. "We've got to get going. We're supposed to meet our friends for dinner at six."

Sylvester prepared the bill on the adding machine. The machine clinked and clacked. Sylvester would make an entry, Hugo would shake his head, said something in Italian, and Sylvester would press a few more keys. The process took almost five minutes. Sylvester handed me the bill. I had so much to drink, I couldn't read it. I handed the bill to Mary Ann and my credit card to Sylvester.

Mary Ann said, "Sylvester, there must be some mistake. The bill is too little for what we ate and drank."

Sylvester smiled. "Hugo insist on family discount."

Somehow, we got home; somehow, we met our friends, the Tarters; somehow, we ate and drink some more. And, somehow, I forgot to mention: while Sylvester and Hugo fell in love in Sicily, Hugo was Hungarian — his father and mother met at a small bar in Budapest after World War II. According to Hugo, it was love at first sight. They were married over 40 years before they perished together in an automobile accident.

Chapter 33

Raging Bull's Eight Wives

DECEMBER 2008

It took 15 years, but I finally had gotten out of the multi-million hole I dug for myself during my ill-fated Wall Street IPO days by sublimating my ego and taking senior management positions at several top advertising agencies.

During my Interpublic Group days in the mid-1990's, I hired a smart, attractive assistant by the name of Taylor. She handled my professional matters flawlessly. In time, she also began to manage the details of our midtown apartment, and saved the Crisci family tens of thousands of dollars in taxes and interest.

First, she got a mortgage modification on our Manhattan apartment to lower our interest rate from 14 percent to seven.

Then she badgered the City of New York to lower our tax assessment, which reduced our real estates taxes by more than 35 percent.

Taylor also became my property manager. To accelerate repayment of accumulated loan guarantees from my IPO days, we had resorted to renting our beloved New York apartment from time to time. She organized some first-class tenants with local brokers: Embassy of Thailand; a wealthy Connecticut-based hedge fund manager who abhorred hotels; and the Transportation Minister for the new Russian Federation.

Taylor quickly discovered, you deal differently with the Russians. Unlike the other tenants that paid by electronic bank transfer, the Russians preferred to pay their rent in cash, in person. Every month Taylor reminded them when their rent was due and arranged a time to meet in my conference room, behind her desk.

"They" were the minster Vladimir and his bodyguard Boris. The two men would show up with an attache full of hundred-dollar bills and count out 45 or 50 depending on the month. Taylor would stand by the door to make sure nobody accidentally interrupted our meeting, then she'd escort them to the front lobby of our offices where a black limousine with black-tinted windows waited to whisk them away.

~

Ten years later, Taylor called out of the blue. "I have an interesting friend you should meet."

"Who is it?" I asked.

She said, "Jake LaMotta, the former middleweight champion of the world."

I remembered watching Jake battle Sugar Ray Robinson at the old Madison Square Garden with Uncle Tip-Top when I was a kid.

"How do you know Jake?"

"Oh, from around," she said.

"And why me?"

"Jake's got a sequel to *Raging Bull*." The film, based on Jake's rise and fall in the boxing business, won a number of academy awards, including best actor for Robert DeNiro. Jake made money as a co-screenwriter and the film's technical advisor.

"Taylor, I don't know anything about the movie business," I replied. *Raging Bull* was such blockbuster, I can't imagine he doesn't have all the Hollywood contacts he'd ever need."

"Just do me the favor," said Taylor impatiently, "You owe me. I told him you were an important business contact he should meet." Taylor was right; I owed her. Besides, it might be a lot of fun. I heard LaMotta was quite a character.

~

We met at LaMotta's favorite restaurant, La Maganette, on 53rd Street near Third Avenue. It looked like a set in a James Cagney gangster movie; the bar and tables were filled with old men and their pay-for-play dates.

Taylor and I arrived first. The guy behind the bar nodded, as if he knew Taylor. We were seated at a quiet table in the rear of the room.

The red-padded front door opened, there stood an aging, well-groomed Jake, now in his 70's, with a knockout blonde and brunette — about 30 years his junior — clinging to his arms. Taylor waved. Jake's entourage started toward us. Literally everybody in the place reached out to shake LaMotta's hand, "Welcome, Champ. Great to see you again, Champ." He loved the recognition. He made a fist and took an imaginary swing. "Looking great, Champ."

Jake hugged Taylor and sat down. He looked me over, "Taylor says you're a hot shot."

"I don't know about that."

He smiled, "Modesty gets you nowhere with the Champ." Two drinks later he was telling stories about his nine legendary fights with Sugar Ray Leonard. How he got robbed more than once; how he showed "them" in the rematches. He placed his hand on the blonde's private parts. She cooed, "Jakey, not in front of wifey." He smiled and put his hand on the brunette's private parts.

Over the next hour, we ate the best veal parmigiana I've ever had — the waiter called it Jake's Way.

Jake started talking business. "Got this sequel screenplay I wrote solo, *Raging Bull 2*. Bedda than the original. Those pricks don't get it."

Some real issues surfaced. During the filming, Jake apparently pissed off everybody — "they couldn't handle the truth." According to Jake, the second problem was — "I ain't in the writers club; so they tell me my new screenplay is shit."

Because Jake was Taylor's contact, I tried to be diplomatic. "Screenplays aren't my area of expertise, but because of my agency connections, I do know a few top commercial directors, and they must have contacts in Hollywood. Mind if I have them take a look? Who knows, maybe you're just a few script changes away from another Academy Award."

He glared angrily. "They can look. But no fuckin' changes."

~

The conversation took a surprising turn. "You married?" he asked. I nodded.

"How long?"

"Forty-six years," I responded.

Jake smiled, "Forty-six for me too." Then he paused. "How many wives?"

"Just one."

"No fuckin' way."

Jake pointed to the brunette — "Jeannie's about to be Number 8, right hon?" He pointed to the blonde — "This is Sheila, she was Number 6. The girls are good friends and they both like veal parmigiana."

I wasn't sure what to say, Taylor filled the void, "So Jeannie, when's the big day?"

"Doesn't really matter. We've ready had the dress rehearsal."

Even Taylor was stumped. "What Jeannie means," said Jake, "is Jeannie was already Number 5. Just didn't work out, right Jeannie?"

"I guess," she responded.

Jake looked at me with fire in his eyes. "After that miserable, scheming Vicki, these girls have been a pleasure."

Sheila smiled, "I treated you good, didn't I, Jakey?"

"Baby, you were a good one. I treated you right." Jake pounded his fist on the table, "Why did you have to screw around with that fuckin' punk?"

"Jakey, this is Jeannie's diner. Let's not," replied Sheila holding Jake's quivering hand. I had now seen LaMota's volatile, intimidating temper up close.

I just stared.

"What the fuck are you looking at, Big Shot," he growled.

I didn't know what to say, so I blurted out something stupid. "I was just wondering."

"Wondering what?"

Taylor eyes opened like saucers. The girls sat silently for what seemed like an eternity. I punted.

"Promise not to swing, Champ?"

His facial expression changed. It was like a lightbulb switched on in his head. He smiled. "You got my word."

"How long are you going to keep doing the marriage thing?"

He leaned across the table. "I'm gonna keep doin' it til I get it right!"

Chapter 34

Mel Brook's Place

APRIL 2010

Selling our apartment in Manhattan after 20 years was like losing a child. But times had changed. Southern California was now our permanent home, our three sons lived there, and we traveled to New York less and less frequently, since a lot of our friends had moved to Florida, South Carolina, and other warm-weather locations.

~

As I sat waiting for the closing to begin, my mind flashed back to the winter of 1990. My oldest son Matt and I were renting an

173

apartment on East 35th Street while Mary Ann wrapped up family matters on the west coast. One Saturday, we were walking over to the East River Heliport on 33rd Street to watch the aircraft take off and land on the tiny pad next to FDR Drive. As we got closer, I noticed a 40-story red granite building with shiny brass trimmings and a giant cloth banner. It read, "Luxury Condos for Sale." It was the only tall building in the immediate area. We walked into a magnificent two-story redwood paneled entrance lobby with couches, sitting areas, and walls filled with original works of art.

The impeccably-dressed receptionist asked, "May I help you?" I responded, "not really, but it looks like a beautiful building."

She did a quick once over. "Maybe you should talk to Ms. King," she said. Like magic, a chic-looking, impeccably-dressed blonde with dark-rimmed glasses stuck her hand out. "Hi, I'm Ruth Ann King, Jensen said you are just looking?" The building was a masterpiece of current technology with cameras and electronic pads everywhere. "It's a little slow today, why don't I just show you a few apartments."

"Ruth Ann, I really don't want to waste your time," I replied.

She pressed on, in a nice sort of way, "The Glick organization has designed the Horizon (building name) to be the ultimate midtown private retreat. It contains a state-of-the-art health club, an on-site tailor, masseuse, pools, yoga rooms, cocktail lounges, and much more.

"It sounds great, but a bit outside my price point."

King knew she was making progress, "So, what is your price point?"

"I don't know, I haven't thought about it. I'm waiting for my wife to return to New York, when Matt's brother (I point to Matt) finishes school in San Francisco."

"I hear private school tuition in San Francisco is as ridiculous as Manhattan."

"That's no lie."

King showed me a paper with a list of apartments and asking prices. I blanched. The one-bedroom, one-bath units started at $671,000. (I didn't realize at the time, but the 1987 market crash had dramatically depressed real estate sales. The city's financial crisis forced real estate taxes to skyrocket and rampant inflation made mortgage rates of 14 percent seemed like a bargain.)

King wasn't about to lose a prospect. She said, "Never know about prices. Mr. Glick is *open to any reasonable offer.*"

I decided it couldn't hurt to look. Matt agreed. "Ruth Ann, what apartment would YOU select? She responded without hesitation, "The J Series. 1,300 square feet (pretty good size for New York), one bedroom, two baths, on a high floor."

I bit, "Why?"

"With a simple modification, it's really a two-bedroom apartment with two full baths. And the high floors have views of the city and bridges from every window."

Ruth Ann was a great salesperson. First she took us through the common areas. We drooled. Then she opened the door to 27 J. The J Unit was exactly as she described. An hour later, we had offered 35 percent of list, agreed on construction modifications, and a wall of floor-to-ceiling mirrors that would bring the New York skyline into the apartment after dark. We also agreed on several other upgrades. "Anything else?" she asked. I was done. She wasn't. "How about we upgrade the kitchen cabinets?"

To my surprise, my lowball bid of $317,00 with improvements was accepted. Days later, Interpublic, delighted they could eliminate their Cricsi rental expense, got a mortgage commitment from their corporate lender, Chase Bank, with a down payment of $3,700 (10 percent), and no points and fees.

I sent Mary Ann the Horizon marketing brochure, and called to congratulate her. I didn't know what to expect, because we had always made major decisions together. She beamed, "What's there not to like? You haven't changed in 25 years — when you see something you want, whether it's your woman or home — you go for it."

~

The Horizon closing was about to begin. The conference was filled mostly with unfamiliar characters on both sides of the table. I imagined the cast of *Blazing Saddles* meeting the cast of *Young Frankenstein.*

My attorney, Karen Martin, whom I had previously only met on the phone, was businesslike and clearly in charge. Karen came highly recommended by my Douglas Elliman real estate agent, Bert Andersen, a sophisticated, well-groomed blonde Swede with a thick accent. Bert also was a recommendation. When the Horizon receptionist, Ellie Switzer, a tough, non-bullshit former sergeant in the Israeli Army, heard we had decided to sell our apartment, she said, sounding like a Gestapo officer, "Bert's your man. Gets the job done. Quick and clean."

Ellie was right. Bert took one walk through our apartment, decorated with one-of-a-kind antiques and artwork collected over the last 30 years. His advice, "Don't change a thing. Figure 60 to 90 days. It's a strong seller's market, and the Horizon is considered an "A" class property.

Bert's estimate turned out to be a bit off. He called seven days later to say he had an all-cash offer 10 percent above the million-dollar asking price. I asked who the buyer was. Bert said, "They don't want publicity. You meet 'em at the closing." I had visions of John Gotti and Bruce Cutler!

Next to Bert was a surly-looking guy in a crumpled suit. Martin Erdleman introduced himself as the title officer. Next to Martin sat an equally undistinguished gentleman, Abe something or other, who said he was the transfer agent, another distinctly New York City-type bureaucrat.

On the other side of the table sat the buyer, actor-producer-director Mel Brooks, his son Mark, and an attorney by the name of Israel Izaac.

"Issy," said Karen, "You know the drill. Any questions on the closing statement?"

Mel interrupted. "I can't pay $1.1 million."

I couldn't believe a guy with all his money wanted to negotiate at the last minute. I thought to myself, only in New York. Karen sensed I was about to blow up the deal; she grabbed my wrist. "Issy, what this all about?"

"Mel explained. He can't pay $1.1 million. What's to hear?"

"I thought we had a firm deal on the purchase price?" glared Karen.

"Just not on paper," replied Issy. Mel smiled and nodded. "You write a million dollars, and Mel has to pay the 10-percent New York millionaire surcharge. Just make the paper $995,000."

"I think it's a bit unusual to ask the seller to reduce the sales price by $105,00 at the last minute."

"Martin, what are you talking about? A deal is a deal with Mel. Just make a side agreement to buy some of the antiques and art in the apartment for the difference. That way Mel is not socked with the extra hundred grand fee."

Karen looked me. "Do you want to sell Mel and Mark your antiques?"

Before I could answer, Issy interrupted, "Martin, we don't want the stuff. Just a paper that says we bought them."

Karen smiled. "Matt, just give me a list of something, I'll attach it as an addendum to the sale."

Two cashier's checks totaling $1.1 million and various signed documents and deeds were passed back and forth across the table.

Issy handed Mark Brooks some keys. "Happy birthday Kid, from your dad." The three of them got up and left. Mel never told a joke or made me laugh, nothing."

Suddenly, Karen was surrounded by vultures seeking checks. The title guy, Edrleman, was the first to present his bill: $4,200. I said, "Why so much? The rates in California — our permanent residence — are half that."

Erdloeman replied, "The apartment is 20 years old. Do you have any idea how long it takes to validate prior owners and verify potential liens?"

"I bought the apartment new, from the developer. I'm the only 27J owner there has ever been."

Erdleman shook his head. "Kiddo, this is New York, the price is the price." He picked his check and walked out the door.

Abe, the transfer agent, was next in line. Karen gave him a check for $8,800. I thought this was highway robbery. Abe looked at me. "I know what you're thinking. You gotta pay the 8 percent on the whole transaction. New York doesn't distinguish between side agreements and contracts."

That left Bert. Karen handed him check for $66,000. "Not bad for a week's work," she said. "I should get that kind of fee."

Bert smiled, "Karen, you know this isn't all mine. I have mouths to feed at Douglas Elliman."

A week later, more bad news. My accountant, Bob Rosenberg called. "I reviewed the closing documents and it looks like you owe the IRS and the State about $149,000 on the sale of the apartment. I suggest we pay them now to avoid potential interest and penalties."

I went ballistic.

He frowned. "You must be joking. You just netted $800,000 on a $32,000 investment and you're complaining?"

Chapter 35

Billie Holiday is Alive and Well

JUNE 2010

The Brooks family was generous. They let us take our time to sort a lifetime of memories that sat in the Horizon apartment.

Since our Southern California home was nearly full, Mary Ann went through a complex process of offering and delivering selected pieces to certain immediate family members. Mitchell wanted the Seventeenth century antique pine armoire from Salisbury, England; niece Elizabeth wanted the glass-topped walnut library table, which had served as a one-of-a-kind dining room table, and so on.

The movers were scheduled to arrive and pack the stuff in the morning. So Mary Ann and I decided to spend one last night in the apartment.

The first thing we did was order a nice Italian meal from a local eatery that delivered. While we waited, we drank a few glasses of wine in the living room and mused about how we acquired some of the furnishings. We laughed about how we shipped the antique Persian rug in the master bedroom from Cairo in 1977, long before most Americans had ever visited the country. A personal Mary Ann favorite was the 200-year-old steamer chest we bought while living in Australia, now a glass-topped coffee table.

~

Joe, our witty, long-time concierge, called on the video phone to announce, "The Last Supper has arrived." The food looked delicious, but the emotions we felt caused us to pick and choose here and there. Mary Ann even left her beloved cannoli partially eaten.

Long ago, I had concluded no Italian meal was complete without a glass of grappa. I went over to the bar and poured myself a glass. I held the bottle up, as if to say, "want one?" Mary Ann pursed her lips, "I've never understood how you can drink that stuff. It look, smells and tastes like turpentine." She opted for a vintage port.

~

On one side of the oversized living room was a 30-foot long expanse of floor-to-ceiling mirrors. The night was crystal clear; the stars twinkled in the mirrors, as did the lights of the 59th Street Bridge over the East River. A few private yachts made their way to the tip of Manhattan Island. It was breathtakingly romantic.

I looked at my beautiful bride of 46 years with her dark brown eyes
surveying the magical New York skyline that stretched from the Empire State Building to the art-deco Chrysler building on 43rd to the illuminated triangle atop the Citicorp headquarters at 53rd and Third, and beyond. She looked exactly like the little teenage girl I met so many years ago. I put my arm around her and whispered, "We may not live here anymore, but New York will always be home."

Time for one last dance. I turned on the stereo, and selected our favorite Billie Holiday album, *Lady Sings the Blues*. The first song up was *You Go to My Head.* As Billie's soulful tones filled the living room, I reached out.; Mary Ann placed her hand in mine; I pulled her close; she put her head on my shoulder.

~

Suddenly it was October 1960. I was at my first college dance. I spotted Mary Ann's sparkling brown eyes for the first time. I asked her for a dance. She gave me her hand, I pulled her close, as we danced to the Lettermen singing *The Way You Look Tonight.* When the music stopped, we exchanged pleasantries. The music began a second time. We danced again.

I walked back over to my friend John who had watched the entire scene. He said, "Well?"

"Her name is Mary Ann and I'm going to marry her."

John laughed cynically. "And I'm going to play centerfield for the New York Yankees." We made a five-dollar bet.

~

Again, June 22, 2010. Mary Ann was still clinging tight after 50 years. My friend John is still one of my best friends, but he never played for the Yankees, and, yes, he still owes me the five dollars.

Recently, I repeated the $5 bet story to another friend and Wall street guru, Ralph Acampora, for the hundredth time. Ralph took out his phone calculator, then looked at me, "Just keep in mind, the present value of that five dollars is $1,199.87."

Chapter 36

Thirty-One Years Ago

MAY 2013

I was in New York promoting my latest book, "Call Sign, White Lily" at the United Nations Book Club. The plan when I finished was to videotape a few recollections of my days at Y&R for the company's upcoming 90th anniversary celebration at their new headquarters at 3 Columbus Circle.

As luck would have it, I was joined by a group of familiar faces from the 60's, 70's and 80's when we worked at the original Y&R headquarters at 285 Madison Avenue. As old people do, we began to reminisce. One of my former creative directors, Bernie Zlotnick, showed us samples of the work he had proudly archived over the decades. The scheduled 30-minute session ran about 90 minutes.

As I was getting ready to leave, I saw a portrait of my old boss and Y&R legend, Chairman Ed Ney, on the wall. I recalled our last discussion in his office 31 years ago like it was yesterday. I asked the anniversary event coordinator, Mary Alice Kennedy, did Ed ever visit the new building. She nodded, "with surprising regularity — in fact he came by so frequently during construction that we decided to call the building the house that Ed built." She took me on a tour. The place was so high tech, I commented "It's like Google on steroids."

Mary Alice laughed. "You're not the first person to say that."

I noticed Ney's portrait on the wall. "I think Ed's here today showing his wife Pat the new digs," said Mary Alice. "Want me to see if he's available?"

"He won't remember me. It was a long time ago."

"Don't be so sure, for 88 he's still got all crackers, and you were quite the rabble-rouser" she said. Mary Alice called Ed's long-time assistant Joanne Carle.

Next thing I know, Joanne called back to say Mr. Ney would like to meet me in the cafe.

I thought, *with all the great people who have walked through the doors of Y&R, I'll be lucky if he even recognizes my face, much less remembers my name.*

I walked into cafe. The always nattily-dressed Ed was sitting at a corner table flanked by Pat and Joanne. He stared, then gave me that Ed Ney wink and raised both arms, "My goodness, Matt Crisci." Then he stood — frailer than I remembered — and gave me a hug. The buttons on my shirt burst; the blood rushed through my veins. I was so pleased, it was hard to maintain my composure.

"Ed, you remembering my name has made my day." I took a deep breath. I've wanted to say something to you for 31 years." It was hard to get the words out. "I want you to know you were my moral compass for 15 years; the Dad I never had."

I was done, but Ed wasn't, "Matt, you've just made <u>my</u> day."

~

It was 1982 all over again. "Remember what I told you when I closed my door?"

I nodded, I could see the door swing shut. He smiled, "I told you to be careful out there. Wall Street was a rough place. How did things turn out?"

"Well, I found out you were right, the hard way. I made a fortune on paper — maybe a hundred and ten million — but thanks to greedy me, I lost everything." Then I paused, "No actually I wound up about $10 million in the hole."

He said knowingly. "But you're still here."

"And how is Mary Ann? I always liked that woman. Never understood what she saw in you."

I had one more question for Ed. "Do you remember Eli Black?"

"You must be joking!"

(Chiquita Bananas affable Chairman Eli Black had hired a new president that had fired Y&R twice before. Ney and Black had an excellent rapport; they agreed I should meet Black in his 44th floor Pan Am Building prior to meeting the new guy. An hour after I left Black's office, he jumped out the window.)

"Always wondered if there was a Matt Crisci cause and effect?" Ed paused. "So what are you doing now?"

"I'm writing books and screenplays."

"That would surprise the hell out of Alex (Alex Kroll). He loved to say, 'there is no such thing as a creative account man.'

"Tell you what, I'd send you a copy of my latest book. You decide.

"What's it called?"

"*This Little Piggy. A Disturbing Tale About Wall Street's Lunatic Fringe*"

What's the storyline?" he asked.

"An arrogant advertising executive who decides to get filthy rich on Wall Street," I responded.

"Sounds vaguely familiar," he smiled.

Three months later, I received a note from Ed saying he enjoyed the book and suggested lunch the next time I was in New York.

Ed passed five months later.

We never had that lunch.

Afterword

I'm not Catholic, Protestant, Muslim, Christian, Jewish or
Hindu.
I am New York.

I'm not American, Italian, Irish, Swedish, Russian or
French.
I am New York.

I'm not Black, White, Asian, Hispanic or Indian.
I am New York.

I'm not heterosexual, straight, gay, lesbian, bisexual or
transsexual.
I am New York.

I'm not 0+, O-, A+ A-, B+, B-, AB+ or AB-.
I am New York.

I'm not introvert-extrovert, obsessive-compulsive, passive-
aggressive, Type A or B.
I am New York.

I'm not leader or follower, extraordinary or ordinary,
worldly or insular.
I am New York.

And, always will be.

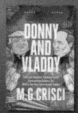